THE COLONNADE OF TEETH

THE COLONNADE
OF TEETH

MODERN HUNGARIAN POETRY

EDITED BY
George Gömöri
& George Szirtes

BLOODAXE BOOKS

ISBN: 1 85224 331 7

First published 1996 by
Bloodaxe Books Ltd,
P.O. Box 1SN,
Newcastle upon Tyne NE99 1SN.

Bloodaxe Books Ltd acknowledges
the financial assistance of Northern Arts.

ACKNOWLEDGEMENTS
Acknowledgements are due to the Arts Council of England
for providing a translation grant for this book. Copyright
acknowledgements are given on pages 269-70.

Funded by
THE
ARTS
COUNCIL
OF ENGLAND

Cover printing by J. Thomson Colour Printers Ltd, Glasgow.

Printed in Great Britain by
Cromwell Press Ltd, Broughton Gifford, Melksham, Wiltshire.

CONTENTS

GYŐZŐ FERENCZ

KEY TO TRANSLATORS

Full details of source books are given in the Acknowledgements on pages 269-70. Translators are credited with the following initials after the poems:

BB	Bruce Berlind
CB	Christine Brooke-Rose
RB	Richard Burns
TC	Tony Connor
JC	János Csokits
DD	Donald Davie
GGo	Gerard Gorman
GG	George Gömöri
TH	Ted Hughes
EJ	Eric Johnson
NK	Nicholas Kolumban
RL	Richard Lourie
KMcR	Kenneth McRobbie
HM	Hugh Maxton
EM	Edwin Morgan
LM	Lucas Myers
ZsO	Zsuzsanna Ozsváth
RS	Robin Skelton
WJS	William Jay Smith
GSz	George Szirtes
DT	Dezső Tandori
CT	Charles Tomlinson
FT	Frederick Turner
AV	Agnes Vadas
VW	Vernon Watkins
DW	David Wevill
CW	Clive Wilmer

FOREWORD

The glory of a language may be its distinctiveness, its individuality, but the downside of this soon makes itself felt if the number of speakers is relatively small. How can the worth of its character and its products be disseminated, if communication is mainly outward-directed and self-suppressive through the native use of major foreign tongues? For many years Hungary had to live with the frustration of knowing it had good poets, and indeed some great poets, whose names were almost unregistered elsewhere. Fortunately this has changed, during the last generation, as editors and poet-translators have made concerted and determined efforts, born of genuine enthusiasm, to recreate Hungarian poems in English, despite the considerable differences in structure between the two languages. This anthology provides an excellent variety of work from poets born between 1900 and 1954.

There are notable poems in many different modes. A personal selection would include 'A Sentence about Tyranny' by Gyula Illyés, where the insidious spread of political oppression into every aspect of life is laid out in cumulative pounding stanzas, at times reminiscent of Auden –

> not just in the door half-open
> and the fearful omen,
> the whispered tremor
> of the secret rumour

– and sometimes strongly suggesting the radical insight of Blake –

> it is the chain slaves wear
> that they themselves prepare...
> in tyranny's domain
> you are the links in the chain

Attila József's 'Night on the Outskirts' is an intensely vivid nocturne of the desolate industrial suburbs of a city: factories like mausoleums, train-whistles, wind-ruffled puddles, taverns heaving out 'fetid light', rags of paper on barren fields, the poet's voice speaking for others:

> Night of the poor, be my coal,
> Smoke here on my heart,
> melt the iron out of me.

Of poems dealing with the fearful disruption of the Second World War, perhaps Miklós Radnóti's 'Forced March' is the most moving: the speaker, on a forced march where the slightest weakness or collapse would be fatal, dreams of home and family and wonders desperately if there can ever be a return:

> Could it perhaps still be? The moon tonight's so round!
> Don't leave me friend, shout at me: I'll get up off the ground!

Obviously, grimness is not all. László Kálnoky in 'The Fatties at the Baths' gives a wonderful picture of the 'stranded slugs' dozing in the steam of a Turkish bath and contemplating the possibility of floating off like balloons 'on a light ray'. Ottó Orbán's brilliant, headlong, unpunctuated *ubi sunt*, 'The Ladies of Bygone Days', must surely banish any lingering thoughts we may have had about the heaviness or overwrought solemnity of (yes, admittedly some) Hungarian poetry:

> Where with their magnetic breasts are Susanna and Martha and the
>   Judys of various addresses
> time has chewed to pulp Melinda and Vera and Liz my god we had
>   breakfast with her bacon and eggs
> Gisella what on earth was her last name gone too gone off on a Danube
>   steamer...

There is much play of words, and play of thought, in the virtuosically varied work of Sándor Weöres, but one of his major poems (excerpted here) 'The Lost Parasol', is an astonishingly imaginative and touching narrative, using the very gradual weathering and disintegration of a red parasol left behind in the countryside by a lover as the focus for a soaring meditation on nature and man's place in it. Equally expansive and impressive is the mythical and yet at the same time paradigmatic anguish of mother and adolescent son in Ferenc Juhász's 'The Boy Changed into a Stag Cries Out at the Gate of Secrets' (excerpted here). These are long poems, loaded with ore, and if anyone feels like murmuring 'too much', contrast lies to hand in the profound pared-down spiritual astringencies of János Pilinszky, with their dark echoes of the Nazi camps and their search for human validity. The troubled but piercing memory of a woman in 'Epilogue' will not readily be forgotten.

Lastly, three poems from younger writers. 'The Perennial Lament' by Zsuzsa Takács uses the black humour of military jargon to convey the classic horror of multiple rape in wartime:

> Beg to report, we have ripped off her shirt!
> Beg to report, we have thrown her on the ground!
> She was sailing like a broken siren.

György Petri's 'Electra' is a short but explosive dramatic monologue where the Greek heroine's desire for revenge is set alight not by admiration for her murdered father Agamemnon but by a Hamlet-like disgust over her mother's preference for her paramour

Aegisthus 'with his trainee-barber's face':

> Even the Sun
> glitters above, like a lie forged of pure gold,
> the false coin of the gods!

And lastly, the beautifully economical and yet mysterious way in which the urban world, the world of nature and its seasons, and the world of human regrets and longings, are brought together in Zsuzsa Rakovszky's 'They Were Burning Dead Leaves' is a fine reminder of how poetry works, in any language:

> To have this again, just this, just the once more:
>   I would sink below
> autumnal earth and place my right hand in your
>   hand like a shadow.

EDWIN MORGAN

INTRODUCTION

The social function of poetry varies from epoch to epoch. During the period of Romanticism poetry was a force for social change, a force so direct that it awoke and articulated a desire for liberation. This desire permeated political structures as much as it did individual consciousness. Poets triggered revolutions, wrote anthems, aspired to become the unacknowledged legislators of the world. Lord Byron and Victor Hugo inspired political activism all over Europe. Among subject nations in particular poetry helped to develop a revolutionary sense of national identity.

All this is commonplace. However, while the twentieth century has seen a diminution of this role in Western Europe, the poem has retained some of its political potency in the smaller Central and Eastern European countries. Hungarians for their part have tended to cling to the belief that poetry can change social life – not the world order perhaps, but their specific conditions and political circumstances. Even Lőrinc Szabó, who could not be called a "committed" poet for the greater part of his life, expressed this conviction when, after the First World War, he defined the poet's task as being 'an instrument of the effective will' (*Legyen a költő hasznos akarat*).

But even in Hungary there are signs that this somewhat anachronistic belief in the political power of poetry is waning. Nevertheless, during our century, it produced a poetry remarkable for its evocative strength and beauty, that addressed the individual as an aesthetic and social being. It treated the reader as a citizen of the world in general, and of Hungary in particular. Whether this latter distinction conferred a blessing or signified a curse the poets could not easily decide, but they agreed that it represented a specific, and often painful condition that could not easily be forgotten. Even the country's linguistic isolation – a Finno-Ugrian language among so much German and Slavic – served as a reminder. It was Endre Ady, the major Symbolist poet of the pre-1914 generation who first formulated the question: 'What is the value of being Hungarian?' (*Mit ér az ember ha magyar?*). Such questions have a peculiar poignancy when asked by Finns, Greeks, Poles or Scots. The problems of small nations are not the same as those of their bigger, and often more fortunate, neighbours.

The history of twentieth-century Hungarian poetry usually assumes the centrality of *Nyugat* (meaning West), a literary magazine which flourished from 1908 through to 1941. According to this account poets are described as being of the first, second or third *Nyugat* generation. A number of the major poets of the first half of the century belong to the second and third generations and they are amply represented here, as are poets who made their reputations after the Second World War. The first generation is not included. We had to draw the line somewhere and we did not want to confront the reader with a large unwieldy book in which the past flourished at the expense of the present. The first and most immediate connection, we felt, would most readily be made with contemporary writing. We therefore decided that only those poets born after 1900 would be included. This meant omitting some excellent poets who are undoubtedly major twentieth-century figures, from Endre Ady through Mihály Babits, Dezső Kosztolányi, Árpád Tóth and Milán Füst. All these are eminently worth reading and by simply mentioning them we hope to signpost future directions translation might take. (Babits particularly looks to be on the point of re-emergence). However, this anthology does not set out to be an objective representation of the best Hungarian poems written this century, but rather to provide a complex, rich and various answer to the questions: how did we get here and where are we now?

In view of this, the poems of Lőrinc Szabó and Attila József assume particular importance since it is they more than anyone who have shaped the course of the second half of the century. Szabó's immersion in everyday speech combined with the formal flexibility of his verse opened up new vistas for those who might otherwise have escaped the influence of the major western modernists (the Hungarian avant-garde remained Lajos Kassák's one-man show, and it was only after his death in 1967 that a younger generation began to apply the lessons of his work). While Szabó experimented with Expressionism, Attila József, in his short life, combined Surrealism with his earlier Classicist and Romantic models to create a poetry that moved between libertarian socialism and the sense of existentialist guilt of his last, most influential poems. One might almost say that János Pilinszky begins his poetic career from that zone of alienation reached by József at the end.

The most memorable poetry of the war years was written by Miklós Radnóti, a modern classicist expressing Judaeo-Christian values in luminous hexameters (Radnóti did not survive the war) and by Gyula Illyés, a populist educated in France. Illyés's poems of the thirties made direct appeals to social conscience, but after the Communist takeover in 1949, his work tended to affirm national and universal values, such as are evidenced by his once banned 'One

Sentence on Tyranny'. This did not prevent some of the poets who were more rigorously silenced in that period regarding him as part of the state establishment and such resentments run deep.

Some poets float above politics, or comprehend them and move on and beyond them. Sándor Weöres eschewed all political creeds and based his poetry on ancient myths and ingenious play-acting. The politics of tyranny are subsumed in these myths and emerge as a kind of redemptive cosmic humour. Wisdom, innocence, passion and experimentalism are all integral to his work and are often simultaneously present in specific poems. We have tried to give some notion of his stature by adapting the title of one of his poems, 'The Colonnade of Teeth', for this anthology. This is, of course, merely a gesture. To some degree our choice of his work, and of others too, is limited by criteria discussed below.

The resentments themselves could fuel an extraordinary energy when combined with classical discipline and a comprehensive vision. This is very much the case with Ágnes Nemes Nagy, who along with János Pilinszky, and Nemes Nagy's husband, the critic Balázs Lengyel, was the driving intelligence of the group associated with the magazine *Újhold* (or New Moon), which was repressed by the authorities on the grounds of bourgeois individualism once the communists seized power. Weöres too was associated with this group as were other fine writers such as the poet László Kálnoky and the novelist Iván Mándy, but Nemes Nagy and Pilinszky are perhaps the two poets who best represent its central tendencies. Nemes Nagy's poetry arises from a curious mixture of the influences of Rilke and, perhaps, Samuel Beckett adapted to a ferocious self-discipline and impersonality. Her 'objective poetry' complements the Catholic existentialism of Pilinszky, whose deepest formative experience was of the death camps he witnessed as one of the first soldiers on the scene afterwards. Compression and concentration, combined with a deep sense of the numinous and sacrificial characterises both poets.

The immediate post-war period produced diverse talents, and if Nemes Nagy and Pilinszky may be taken as leading examples of what became known as the Urbanist (*urbánus*) tendency, Ferenc Juhász and László Nagy, with their peasant background, represent the Populist or Ruralist (*népies*) element, which both in literary politics and in politics at large, has appeared as the expression of an alternative national consciousness, or, more accurately perhaps, as an alternative partly by virtue of its more conscious adoption of national consciousness. Urbanist and Populist values represent a dichotomy in Hungarian society, as much in the adoption of a 'western and intellectual' versus a 'national and instinctive' identity as in the approach to specific poetic problems, such as metre and imagery. The rich imagery of Juhász and Nagy, which draws upon both the magic transformations of folk tales and the dislocations of modern life as expressed in Surrealism and Expressionism, attempts what is sometimes called the Bartókean synthesis, and was, in the early days of Hungarian Stalinism, harnessed into the service of social and political change, fuelling the antagonism between the rival cultural forces. Juhász's most productive period was the mid-fifties and early sixties, while László Nagy's best work dates belongs to the ten years following.

After the 1956 revolution, an event of enormous and problematic significance in Hungarian history (a significance still to be resolved) many Hungarians fled to the West and new avenues of experience opened before them. Győző Határ and György Faludy are the oldest and most distinguished representatives of this strange species (the most recent volume of Határ's autobiography refers to the writer as a 'Stranded Whale'), an enormously talented generation who have lived or are still living in their adopted countries but who write in their native tongue. Their re-absorption in the Hungarian tradition following the political events of 1989 is incomplete, and will probably remain that way for some time. As for the large Hungarian ethnic minority in present-day Romania, it has produced eminent poets from the tragically short-lived Jenő Dsida to Sándor Kányádi whose voice became a rallying point for moral resistance in the worst years of the Ceaucescu regime. The dramatic intensity of Kányádi's work, and of other Hungarian Transylvanian poets, is an indication of the pressures under which a community survives severe linguistic and cultural discrimination.

Post-modernism has not affected Hungarian poetry in any significant way yet. While Dezső Tandori's early work broke new ground it did not establish a path clear enough to be followed by disciples. The two most interesting poets of the post-1968 period, György Petri and Zsuzsa Rakovszky, achieved their present status by resisting the conformism-within-diversity imposed by the Kádár régime. Where Petri took to *samizdat* and direct political comment, Rakovszky's poetry established a persona that appeared introspective but in fact registered the realities of Hungarian society on its highly sensitive pulse. Petri's influences include Eliot, Cavafy and Gottfried Benn. A lyrical poet deliberately gone sour, he is also a highly effective and accomplished satirist. Rakovszky is more influenced by American and English models such as Emily Dickinson and Carol Ann Duffy.

This anthology is not primarily about national obsessions – it simply presents what the editors consider to be, if not unarguably the best, then at least the best translated poetry written by Hungarian poets born in the specified period. In view of this they do not expect a ready critical consensus, at least on the Hungarian side. Some outstanding poets are notoriously difficult – Weöres particularly – and while both editors consider him extraordinary by any measure, they believe it does his case more harm than good to present his work in unsatisfactory translation. This is the natural limitation of all translated work. Weöres lives so thoroughly in the nooks and crannies of the language and is so inventive in various forms from nonsense rhyme to rhapsodic verse that to lift any one part of him from the whole implies a distortion. For the time being his true essence is locked into its Hungarian mode of saying. One might add that this works both ways of course, and that, for various reasons, the reputations of Auden, Graves and Larkin in Hungary are based on hearsay rather than on hard Hungarian evidence.

Of the poets represented in this anthology fourteen are dead, twenty-one still alive and writing. Omissions are the hardest. All anthologies of recent work, whether in translation or not, are necessarily interim assessments and the reader should take particular care to bear this in mind here, where the impression gained of the nature of scope of individual writers is so conditional. At the same time we feel there is a great diversity of voices here, all worth listening to, each representing an enrichment of our store and expectations of poetry. For a non-Hungarian speaker we intend the primary experience to be pleasure and excitement. For us, as individual editors, we regard the final result as the sum and overlap of our individual enthusiasms.

GEORGE GÖMÖRI
& GEORGE SZIRTES

LŐRINC SZABÓ

The Dreams of the One

Since you are this way and they are that
and his interests are different
and truth's a sort of nervous fact
or verbal front
and since nothing out there pleases me
and since the crowd still has supremacy
and of the framing of rules I am utterly
innocent:
it is high time now
that I escaped your net.

What should I go on waiting for any longer,
timidly scanning days to come?
Time hurries past, and whatever lives
is true to itself alone.
Either I am sick, or you are; and
am I not to recognise the weapons in the hand
of love or hate that comes to stand
before my face?
If I am forever only to understand,
where is my own place?

No! no! no! How can I bear to be
no more than a thread in a mad web:
to understand and honor the guard
and share his pain, his pain!
All who could, have long got out of the snares,
they go freely through and about the wires.
I and the world, there go the two of us,
captive in the cage,
the world with the limelight on itself,
like me on my own stage.

We're escaping, my soul, we've sprung the lock,
the mind has leapt away
but is careful to paint itself
with the bars of appearance.
Inside it is one that outside's a thousand fragments!

Who knows where the man ever went
that saw the fish, and still the net
intact?
Forbidden? By someone else! Sin? To them,
if caught in the act!

Within us, inside, no divisions or frontiers,
nothing is forbidden;
we are only what we are, each one a solitude,
not bad, not good.
Hide in the depths of yourself! For there,
the great and free dream, you'd swear,
lies abandoned still, as where
our mother the unbounded
sea appears like a memory
in the sharp taste of our tears and blood.

Back into the sea, into ourselves! Only
where we can be free!
We needn't look out yonder to see
anything coming to us from the Many.
If ever we are hucksters with the crowd,
truth crumbles down to powder;
Only the One is our home ground,
never undone:
let us dream, if we still can,
the dreams of the One!

[EM]

Farewell
(from Cricket Music)

What happened? My dear, don't cry. The thing
I felt was: moulting. There's been a dissolving
of the threads in my fate, and now I am spun
by a hundred spaces and times (in the old days one),

destroying-and-building. Turtle-doves coo up there,
have sung four days above me; but I'd despair
of telling you fearful wars have raged here too.
Even to myself it is hard to believe this is true,
although my senses branch out each minute. Your pain
is new, looks through me, asks where I remain.
In a million places every inch of me!
What is it then? Love, electricity?
I'm in the dark still. Maybe gold-gas-atom,
maybe heat-ray-nucleus. Light on Saturn,
space-living light. It's strange. But that
the Universe is only a Poet's Brain I grant
seems true. – Are you going? I feel night's touch.

[EM]

Heart Attack in Tihany

It came at five minute intervals. The pill
was useless now. Cramp followed cramp. And still
they came. At ten could feel my heart contract
within a ring of pain, was choked and racked;
from ten o'clock lay half dead while the ache
coiled through my body like an iron snake,
up temples, down the arms, beyond control,
in furious search of one magnetic pole,
hanging upon that lodestar, dangling clear
on one thin nerve, a great dead weight of fear;
my only line to earth, that fraying strand
was everything: all I could understand
was my own pain. My loves and friends looked on
like helpless witnesses. I wished them gone
and told them so. By dawn a change set in
a vague relief, a gentle humming din,
morning: the lake, the hill. I saw the sun...
(October 10th it was, in '51.)

[GSz]

Reaction

I watched the comedy right through.
My hair greyed in the process.
It said each man's a hooligan,
Each woman a psychosis.

My belly and mind have had enough
My mouth is bitter from it.
You want reaction, life? You rise
in my throat like vomit.

[GSz]

Ice

There is a kind of pain as cold as ice.
Have you not burned your hands on a frozen
door-knob? So the hard frost of nausea
settles on the spirit, encrusts, grips like a vice,
spikes and squeezes out the high explosive fury,
and so, however hot, the flaming sun
can lie benumbed under its heavy burden,
grow just as numb, so gripping it will burn you.
A poem can be colder than the ice,
cold as the icy moon: did you see it
glittering in the sky this February night?
It was lovely! Its song, as hushed as glass,
was the rustling of the starlit universe...
My heart too burns and glitters. Just like ice.

[GSz]

Listening to Mozart

'I count only the hours of joy,' it said,
inscribed under the sundial, and I read
the ornamental Latin, envying
in misery the scholar who could sing
so cheerfully and cut such words into
unfeeling granite, though for all I knew
a quip was all it was, a whimsy caught
on a light breeze and frozen into thought.
Resolution, whim: such states of mind
were once my style, but darkness, being blind,
obscured the light. I should have stuck at it
and probed the clouds to find that ball of wit,
unlocked the floodgates and let loose a tide
of golden sunlight for my joy to ride,
one mayfly moment where my youthful ardour
might have found a temporary harbour,
a grace now gone, whose sharpened knife has spilt
so much of my blood since in bouts of guilt.
Spirit-like, swift, it still stabs at the heart,
with fierce desire, like dragonflies that dart
in blue glazed fires, in double loops, in throes
of passionate coupling, now far off, now close,
from flaming noons straight through into the night,
and I am flying with them, sparkling, bright,
under sharp stars, by pond and weed and stones,
as young as they, aged only in my bones
(though monstrous truth within me scoffs and moans)
knowing it is specifically that gift
of floating free, that light and childhood drift
I should recover and have at my shift,
reclaiming it along with water sprites
and dragonflies, and henceforth set my sights
upon that timeless course and timeless sky
where I'd be governed, as I have been, by
the power of images, upraised, diffused,
precisely as the baton used
by a conductor raises him when in one sweep
he raises bass and cello from the deep!

Yes, that's the very thing, that bright day steeped
in scented dancing, in those fawnlike capers
light as air in a vivid froth of vapours,
that clear blue air is what I should recapture
so I should feel their freshness, heat and rapture;
yes, rather that, than share with polar bears
and walruses the thorough chill which tears
their flesh, poor beasts (resembling me) who yearn
for hells and fires where they might ever burn.
So, fearful of their terrors, listening
to Mozart's music, I consider spring
and summer, (both now past, although they too
had seen, old buffers, fifty-five years through!)
and sigh in hope to Music, *make me young!*
as young as you, sweet painful rhythm flung
into enchantment, fluting and supplying
enough of hope to save the fire from dying:
you are the shadow caught within a beam
of brilliant heart calming light, the stream
of sparkling sun that burns like grains of glass
beneath the sea green boughs along the grass,
yours is the wisdom and the ripe old age
possessed by him, under whose patronage
was carved the motto – 'Non numero horas
nisi serenas!' to shelter and restore us,
whose admonition time failed to destroy:
who counts, he claims, 'only the hours of joy'.

[GSz]

Moments

Ever since I kissed you last night and you
permitted (if only for a moment
before protesting) my knee to rest between
your own two passionately trembling knees
my mind in its state of grace keeps conjuring
your image: standing before me at work,
or out in the street bumping into you:
your head tipped back, cheeks glowing, your eyes closed,
lips lovely with that beatific smile
of agonised desire. Seeing this, I too
close my eyes for a moment and feel dizzy.
I sense you close to me, my face bathed in
the tender lines of your face, your hot breasts
burning my palms, you're kissing me again,
and I wake up in a sweat: surely this
is madness – and yet how good it feels to lose
myself within you, to feel your body
like a deluge rushing about me and I
galloping fast through the powerful current
of you as you billow and part before me.

[GSz]

GYULA ILLYÉS

The Apricot Tree

1

The apricot tree
shoulder-high or less –
Look! an apricot
at branch-tip ripeness.

Stretching, straining,
holding out a prize,
the tree is a maiden
offering closed eyes.

You stand and wonder:
will she bend and sway
her slender waist or
step back, run away.

With quick breath shudders
from heat or passion,
fans herself, signals
in the high fashion,

Shakes the shimmering
pomp out of her dress;
then blushing, she waits
for your compliments.

This garden a ballroom,
she gazes about,
anxiously, constantly,
wants to be sought out.

2

I spend each evening,
all evening with her.
'Come again tomorrow'
she says in whisper.

She rustles softly
when I salute her.
It seems my poetry
can still transmute her.

Sweet apricot tree,
in a dream I saw
the cool arbour, and you
on the crackling straw.

First you glanced around
anxiously, then left
the dark hedge, the well,
in your moon-white shift.

Your stepping increased
the silence gently,
brought me your body
soft and sweet-scented.

Since that dream I glance
towards you, flushing.
Please look at me too,
askance and blushing.

[CB]

Rivers, Fjords, Small Villages...

Waterloo, Wagram, Mohi – what were they
Before their mild and empty names were filled
With keenings and a thousand deaths, went sailing
Away to shell the overcast? Unskilled
We were in you, in fjord, hamlet, field
And equable river. And your fate incurred
Ought to have been, and ought to be today,
              To persevere unheard.

But thus the earth expands. New meadowlands,
New mountains in the mind of the child at school
Rise where gunbarrels probe the map and point
To what they meant, being devastation's fool,
To erase from earth. The gun's a new ferrule
For the geography master, bright and burning
Milestone on the one old road that bends
                Towards one more turning.

One more, mankind? I who walked trusting by
Your side, now stand apart. Or do I plead
Against the tide, standing upon some whirled
Shipboard? If sin on sin is all the seed
Your learning sows, why then, my kind, indeed
Your servitude of spirit has to be
(An envious god's curse) endless. I shall cry
                As long as I can, my plea.

Be mute, Petsámo, bay and virgin hill
And you, secluded vales and homesteads; hounds
Couched to await a carcass like Sedan!
And you, small isles where Death the discoverer grounds
His keel, and an undreamed-of epoch founds!
Small places, new Americas, so long
Doomed to great fame, whose ruinous bounties swell,
                Be mute – nay, howl! Give tongue!

And see your destiny through. Come brighten, burn
As so many new stars! Ranked in armies, make
Not only history to a new design
But a new geometry on a sky in wreck.
And you, Petsámo, lurid bloody speck,
Rise, a new dispensation, on our sight:
That some time Man, in time to come, shall turn
                More hopefully, to the height...

[DD]

Grass Snake and Fish

Among pebbles, at the pond's edge,
   in limpid shallows whose water
flows as transparent as the atmosphere,
   suddenly visible

in that world made for other lungs,
   living purity, where
the stone wavers in the drift
   of the reflection, a branch in air;

into that shut Eden, slides the snake,
   guided by the oldest law:
a fish palpitates hanging from its fangs
   howling what no one can translate.

[CT]

A Sentence About Tyranny

Where tyranny exists
that tyranny exists
not only in the barrel of the gun
not only in the cells of a prison

not just in the interrogation block
or the small hours of the clock
the guard's bark and his fists
the tyranny exists

not just in the billowing black fetor
of the closing speech of the prosecutor,
in 'the justified use of force'
the prisoners' dull morse

not merely in the cool postscript
of the expected verdict
there's tyranny
not just in the crisp military

order to 'Stand!' and the numb
instruction 'Fire!', the roll of the drum,
in the last twitch
of the corpse in the ditch

not just in the door half-open
and the fearful omen,
the whispered tremor
of the secret rumour

the hand that grips,
the finger before the lips,
tyranny is in place
in the iron mask of the face

in the clench of the jaw
the wordless O
of pain and its echo
and the tears

of silence-breeding fears,
in the surprise
of starting eyes

tyranny supplies
the standing ovation, the loud
hurrahs and chanting of the crowd
at the conference, the songs

of tyranny, the breasts
that tyranny infests,
the loud unflagging
noise of rhythmic clapping,

at opera, in trumpet cry,
in the uproarious lie
of grandiose statues, of colours.
in galleries,

in the frame and the wash,
in the very brush,
not just in the neat snarl
of the midnight car

as it waits
outside the gates

tyranny permeates
all manners and all states,
its omnipresent eyes more steady
that those of old Nobodaddy,

there's tyranny
in the nursery
in father's advice, in his guile,
in your mother's smile

in the child's answer
to the perfect stranger;

not just in wires with barbs and hooks
not just in rows of books,
but, worse than a barbed wire fence
the slogans devoid of sense

whose tyranny supplies
the long goodbyes;
the words of parting,
the will-you-be-home-soon, darling?

in the street manners, the meetings
and half-hearted greetings,
the handshakes and the alarm
of the weak hand in your palm,

he's there when your loved one's face
turns suddenly to ice
he accompanies you
to tryst or rendezvous

not just to the grilling
but to the cooing and the billing,
in your words of love he'll appear
like a dead fly in your beer

because even in dreams you're not free
of his eternal company,
in the nuptial bed, in your lust
he covers you like dust

because nothing may be caressed
but that which he first blessed,
it is him you cuddle up to
and raise your loving cup to

in your plate, in your glass he flows
in your mouth and through your nose
in frost, fog, out or in
he creeps under your skin

like an open vent through which
you breathe the foul air of the ditch
and he lingers like drains
or a gas leak at the mains

it's tyranny that dogs
your inner monologues,
nothing is your own
once your dreams are known

all is changed or lost,
each star a border post
light-strafed and mined; the stars
are spies at window bars,

the vast tent's every lamp
lights a labour camp,
come fever, come the bell
it's tyranny sounds the knell,

confessor is confession,
he preaches, reads the lesson
he's Church, House and Theatre
the Inquisition;

you blink your eyes, you stare
you see him everywhere;
like sickness or memory
he keeps you company;

trains rattling down the rail
the clatter of the jail;
in the mountains, by the coast
you are his breathing host;

lightning: the sudden noise
of thunder, it's his voice
in the bright electric dart,
the skipping of the heart

in moments of calm,
in chains of tedium,
in rain that falls an age,
the star-high prison-cage

in snow that rises and waits
like a cell, and isolates;
your own dog's faithful eyes
wear his look for disguise,

his is the truth, the way
so each succeeding day
is his, each move you make
you do it for his sake;

like water, you both follow
the course set and the hollow
ring is closed; that phiz
you see in the mirror is his

escape is doomed to failure,
you're both prisoner and gaoler;
he has soaked, corroded in,
he's deep beneath your skin

in your kidney, in your fag,
he's in your every rag,
you think: his agile patter
rules both mind and matter

you look, but what you see
is his, illusory,
one match is all it takes
and fire consumes the brake

you having failed to snuff
the head as it broke off;
his 'vigilance' extends
to factories, fields and friends

and you no longer know or feel
what it is to live, eat meat or bread
to desire or love or spread
your arms wide in appeal;

it is the chain slaves wear
that they themselves prepare;
you eat but it's tyranny
grows fat, his are your progeny

in tyranny's domain
you are the link in the chain,
you stink of him through and through,
the tyranny IS you;

like moles in sunlight we crawl
in pitch darkness, sprawl
and fidget in the closet
as if it were a desert,

because where tyranny obtains
everything is vain,
the song itself though fine
is false in every line,

for he stands over you
at your grave, and tells you who
you were, your every molecule
his to dispose and rule.

[GSz]

Tilting Sail

The tilting sail careens;
   scything the foam,
the tall mast creaks and leans –
   the boat plows on.

Look – when do mast and sail
   fly forward most
triumphantly? When tilted
   lowest.

[WJS]

At the Turning Point of Life

Night envelops us: clouds rest, darkness drizzles –
outside, the branches are bare and glittering wet;
as the wind sweeps by, they let fall their tears –
youth is passing.

Before my window two swallows dive, dip down,
almost hand in hand like fish at the bottom of the sea.
One is love, I thought, and the other, secret hope.
All that accompanied me flees, quietly retreating to a truer homeland.

And now in her loose robes, with large, disproportionate
limbs, monster Melancholy sits down beside me,
drawing my head to her moist breast,
and mocks me: 'Weep if you dare, weep, unhappy one…

Mourn if you have anything to mourn for: Examine your life:
Around you autumn rain pours down and mist covers the wooded
      hills;
frothy, filthy water rushes toward you down the sloping road
where once with secret intent you led your beloved.'

Like prayer beads drops run down the windowpane.
O you nimble minutes, seasons, centuries: – autumn twilight
        covers the paper
over which I lean as to a mirror, twilight that soon will cover my
        young face.
Through trickling drops I watch the brown trees swing, reaching
        into the mist.

[WJS]

ATTILA JÓZSEF

Mother

All this last week I have been thinking
of my mother, thinking of her taking
up in her arms the creaking basket
of clothes, without pausing, up to the attic.

Oh I was full of myself in those days –
shouting and stamping, crying to her to leave
her washing to others, to take me in place
of the basket, play with me under the eaves –

But calmly she went on, lifting out the clothes,
hanging them to dry, she had no time to scold
or even to glance at me, and soon the line
was flying in the wind, white and clean.

I cannot shout now – how could she hear?
I see her, great, vast, yet somehow she is near.
The wet sky shines washed with her blue,
her grey hair streams where the clouds scud through.

[EM]

Grief

In my eyes grief dissolves;
I ran like a deer;
Tree-gnawing wolves
In my heart followed near.

I left my antlers
A long time ago;
Broken from my temples,
They swing on a bough.

Such I was myself:
A deer I used to be.
I shall be a wolf:
That is what troubles me.

A fine wolf I'm becoming.
Struck by magic, while
All my pack-wolves are foaming,
I stop, and try to smile.

I prick up my ears
As a roe gives her call;
Try to sleep; on my shoulders
Dark mulberry leaves fall.

[VW]

Welcome to Thomas Mann

Just as the child, by sleep already possessed,
Drops in his quiet bed, eager to rest,
But begs you: 'Don't go yet; tell me a story,'
For night this way will come less suddenly,
And his heart throbs with little anxious beats
Nor wholly understands what he entreats,
The story's sake or that yourself be near,
So we ask you: Sit down with us; make clear
What you are used to saying; the known relate,
That you are here among us, and our state
Is yours, and that we all are here with you,
All whose concerns are worthy of man's due.
You know this well: the poet never lies,
The real is not enough; through its disguise
Tell us the truth which fills the mind with light
Because, without each other, all is night.
Through Madame Chauchat's body Hans Castorp sees,
So train us to be our own witnesses.

Gentle your voice, no discord in that tongue;
Then tell us what is noble, what is wrong,
Lifting our hearts from mourning to desire,
We have buried Kosztolányi; cureless, dire,
The cancer on his mouth grew bitterly,
But growths more monstrous gnaw humanity.
Appalled we ask: More than what went before,
What horror has the future yet in store?
What ravening thoughts will seize us for their prey?
What poison, brewing now, eat us away?
And, if your lecture can put off that doom,
How long may you still count upon a room?
O, do not speak, and we can take heart then.
Being men by birthright, we must remain men,
And women, women, cherished for that reason.
All of us human, though such numbers lessen.
Sit down, please. Let your stirring tale be said.
We are listening to you, glad, like one in bed,
To see today, before that sudden night,
A European mid people barbarous, white.

[VW]

Night on the Outskirts

Our kitchen fills with dusk
like an underwater pit.
Up through the narrow court
light slowly lifts its net.

Silence. The scrub brush torpidly
seems to get its legs and move.
Above, a section of the wall
ponders whether it will fall.

And on the sky in oily rags
night pauses and emits a sigh,
crouches at the city's edge,
then stirs and, wobbling through the square,
sets aflame a piece of moon.

The factories stand like ruins.
And yet within
the deeper darkness
the pedestal of silence
is being forged.

On the windows of the textile mill
moonbeams drift in bundles.
The moon's soft light is thread
across the ribs of looms.
Work has stopped till morning
but the falling dreams of factory girls
weave restlessly
on the machines.

Beyond,
like a vaulted mausoleum:
iron, cement works, factories for bolts,
echoing family crypts.
The workshops guard the secret
of sombre resurrection
and a cat
scratches at the fence of boards.

The superstitious watchman sees
a glimmering light, the will-o'-the-wisp.
The dynamoes
like insect backs
coldly gleam.

The whistle of a train.
Dampness rummages the gloom
in the foliage of a fallen tree
and weights the dust along the road.

A policeman's on the road
and a mumbling worker.
Here and there a comrade,
clutching leaflets, scurries past,
sniffing ahead like a dog,
listening behind like a cat.
Every streetlamp's his detour.

The tavern mouth heaves fetid light,
the tavern windows vomit puddles.
Inside, a lamp swings, guttering,
and while the tavern keeper snores
a lone day labourer stands watch.
He bares his teeth against the wall.
His pain is bubbling up the stairs.
He cries. He cheers the revolution.

The crackling water hardens
like cooling ore.
Like a stray dog, the wind is walking,
his big tongue lolls and touches water,
swallows water.
Mattresses of straw like rafts
are swimming on the currents of the night.

The warehouse is a grounded boat,
the foundry is an iron barge,
and the iron-smelter dreams
of a scarlet infant in the moulds.

Everything is damp. Eveything is heavy.
Mildew maps the countries
of misey on the walls.
Out in the barren fields
rags and bits of paper
lie on the ragged grass –
how they would like to crawl!
They stir but have
no power to move...

O night, the replica
of your damp and clinging wind
flitters in the dirty sheets.
You're hanging in the sky
like ripped cloth on a dress,
like pain on life, O night!
Night of the poor, be my coal,
smoke here on my heart,
melt the iron out of me,
the standing, unsplit anvil,
hammer flashing, clanging –
gliding blade for victory,
O night!

The night is grave, the night is heavy.
Brothers, I too will sleep.
May suffering not lie upon our souls
and on our bodies may no vermin feed.

[LM/AV]

Without Hope

Slowly, broodingly

All you arrive at in the end
is a sad, washed-out, sandy plain,
you gaze about, take it in, bend
a wise head, nod; hope is in vain.

Myself, I try to look about
nonchalantly, without pretence.
Axe-arcs shake their silver out
rippling where the aspens dance.

My heart sits on the twig of nothing,
its little body shivering, dumb.
One calm unbroken gathering,
staring, staring, the stars come.

In an iron-coloured sky

The chilly, lacquered dynamo
rotates in an iron-coloured sky.
Silent constellations! Oh
how my teeth make speech-sparks fly –

The past drops through me like a rock
through space – not a sound there.
Time drifts, a blue unticking clock.
Sword-metal flares out: but my hair –

My moustache settles, a gorged caterpillar,
over a mouth numbed of all taste.
My heart's in pain, words come chillier,
Words with no listener are a waste –

[EM]

Dead Landscape

The water smokes, the bulrushes
sag and wilt into the wilderness.
The sky cowers deep in its quilt.
Thick silence cracks in the snow-filled
        field.

Gross and greasy the silent sundown;
flat the plain, featureless and round.
Only a single barge, heard
slapping self-absorbed on the furred
        lake.

Newborn time rattles in the cold
branches of the icy wood.
Chittering frost finds some moss here,
ties up its skeletal horse here
    to rest.

Then the vines. And among them plums.
Damp straw on the stocks and stumps.
And a procession of thin stakes,
good for old peasants' walking-sticks
      in the end.

A croft – this countryside revolves
all round it. Winter with its claws
keeps cracking plaster till it falls
in pieces from the homestead walls:
      cat's-play.

The pigsty door gapes wide open.
It sags and creaks, the wind's playpen.
What if a sucking-pig trots in
and a field of corn should sport and spin
      on the cob!

The room small, the peasants small.
Dried leaves in the smoker's bowl.
For these ones, no prayer will work.
They sit there, deep in the dark,
      thinking.

The vines are freezing for the landlord.
His is the crackling of the wood.
His is the pond and under its ice
it is for him the good fish hides
      in the mud.

[EM]

Ode

1

Here I sit on a shining wall.
The light young summer wind
rises like the warm welcome of supper.
I accustom my heart to the silence:
not hard.
Here
I regain what I lost,
I bend my head,
my head hangs down.

My eyes are on the mane of the mountains –
your splendid brow,
every leaf on fire!
On the street no one, no one;
I see your skirt lifted by the wind.
Your hair strays under fine leaves,
I see your soft breasts
trembling –
as Szinva brook runs down –
Oh what I see:
a magic laugh
shining on your teeth,
on the round white stones.

2

Oh how I love you!
You have been able to force
speech from the universe –
and from solitude, weaving its fitful deceits
in the heart's deepest place.
Now, as the booming leaves the waterfall,
you leave, you run subdued, until
I cry from among the peaks of life, singing
in those distances hung between earth and heaven,
that I love you, that it is you,
sweet would-be mother that I love.

3

I love you as the child loves its mother,
as the silent cave loves its depths.
I love you as rooms love sunlight,
as the soul loves warmth and the body rest.
I love you as mortal men love living
and strive in its arms till death.

I am the keeper of your words, your smiles,
your moments – everything, as the earth keeps
everything that falls.
My instincts, like acid on metal, have
engraved you on my mind; my existence
takes form at last, dear love, from your sweet essence.

Loudly the moments pass by;
dumb you remain, dumb, and I
have ears for you alone.
Glittering stars – already they are setting,
but you are always steady in my sight.
Breath of silence in the cave: your flavour
stings cold in the mouth; at times your hand
with its delicate veining will bend
mistily round the glass of water.

4

Oh but what substance am I made of,
moulded and carved by your simplest glance?
What mind, what light and miracle
that can make me reach the gentle
dales of your fertile
body, through the mist of absence?

As the word is released by reason,
I can delve into your enigmas!...

Your veins quiver like bushes,
ceaselessly, bushes of roses.
They move in the undying stream,
for love to flourish in your face
and your belly to bear its fruit.

The sensitive soil of your flesh
is sown with finest roots,
thin threads it knots, unknots, –
for the juices of the tiny cells
to crowd to a growing mass,
and the leafy bush of the lungs
to murmur up its praise!

And the deep undying matter advances
singing in its galleries, and rich life emerges
from tireless wells, from the very scourings
of buried pits, of burning kidneys!

In you, the swelling hills
rise, constellations wink,
lakes move, and workshops work:
a million beings, quick
insects,
bladderwrack,
cruelty and goodness;
suns shine, auroras go dark –
here, in your huge essence,
the eternal unconscious wanders.

5

Like clotted blood, in shreds,
these words
are dropped in your path.
Existence stammers:
only law has a clear voice.
My active senses, reborn day after day,
are ready even now
for silence.

But up to now everything cries aloud –
chosen out of two thousand millions,
you alone, you the living bed,
you the gentle cradle, you the fierce tomb:
into yourself: into yourself I
beseech you, receive me.

(How deep the sky at daybreak!
Armies shine in light of steel.
The glitter hurts my sight.
I am lost, in this air.
Surely my heart must break,
beating in the light.)

6 *After-song*

(The train takes me, I follow after you,
perhaps today I'll find you again,
perhaps my burning face will be cool,
perhaps you'll say, in your undertone:

The water's lukewarm, go and try it!
A towel for your body, dry it!
The meat is baked, end your hunger!
In my bed for ever linger.)

[EM]

Elegy

Smoke, under a low leaden sky, swirls hooded
in thick banks over the sad land:
and so my soul, back and forward,
sways like the smoke.
Sways, yet stays.

Iron soul you are – yet tender in images!
Going behind the heavy tread of the real,
look deep into yourself, see
where you were born!

– Here, under a sky once supple and flowing
across the loneliness of thin dividing
walls, where the menacing, impassively imploring silence
of misery slowly loosens the melancholy
so solidly
packed in the thinker's heart
and mingles it with the heart
of millions.

The whole dominion of men
begins here. Here everything is a ruin.
A tough euphorbia has spread
its umbrella over the abandoned factory yard.
Into a damp darkness
the days go down by stained steps
from shatter of paltry windows.
Tell me:
is it here you are from?
Here, where you are tied to your gloomy wish
to be like other wretched souls
in whom this age, the great age, is
straitjacketed: the others whose faces
are marked by every line that's made?

Here you rest, here where the rickety creak
of a fence still guards the greed
of the moral order,
and watches it all.
Can you recognise yourself? Here the souls
wait in a void for the towering beauty-filled
future, as the dark and desolate shacks
have dreams of houses, lifting high
a nimble web of murmurs. Set
in the dried mud, fragments of glass
stare with fixed eyes, cut off from the light,
over the tortured meadow-grass.

From the low hills a thimble
of sand rolls down at random…and there's a flash,
a buzz of some fly – black, green, or blue –
attracted here from richer neighbourhoods
by the rags,
by the leavings of man.

Good is mother earth, tormented in her care,
also in her way
preparing a table.
A yellow weed springs in a saucepan there!

What have you to say
to this dry heart's-leap of recognition which draws me –
to a landscape that is bone of my bone?
What of my rich torment – coming back, back here?
So a mother's son,
after the cudgels of strangers, will return.
Here, only here, you may smile and cry, and
here, here only, can your sinew endure,
my soul! This is my native land.

[EM]

In Light, White Clothes

I have chewed it all and spat it out,
everything that is not my food.
Up there, I neither care nor doubt:
soap-bubble or empyrean vault?
I know what is and is not good.

And like a little child, I know
only playing brings happiness.
I have so many games to show;
reality always turns to go,
appearance lives in steadiness.

The rich can have no love for me
as long as I am poor like this.
And the poor, I leave them equally
cold, how could I be consolatory
where love comes shameful and amiss?

I am the creator of my own love...
Star and planet feel my tread:
I set out for the gods above,
in opposition – heart calm enough –
in light, white clothes striding ahead.

[EM]

'Well, in the End I Have Found My Home...'

Well, in the end I have found my home,
the land where flawless chiselled letters
guard my name above the grave
where I'm buried, if I have buriers.

It will take me like a collecting-box,
this earth. For no one (sadly) wants
wartime leftovers of base metal,
wretched devalued iron coins.

Or an iron ring engraved
with noble words: new world, rights, land.
Our laws are still the fruit of war;
gold rings shine finer on the hand.

For many years I was alone.
Then all about me was a crowd.
It's up to you, they said, although
I'd have loved to follow them round.

It was like that, empty, the way I lived:
no one has to tell me it was.
I was compelled to play the fool
and now I die without a cause.

In that whole whirlwind of my life
I have tried to stand my ground.
More sinned against than sinning, I
leave that thought and laugh aloud.

Spring is beautiful, summer too,
autumn better, winter the best
when you leave your hopes for family
and hearth to other men at last.

[EM]

JENŐ DSIDA

Maundy Thursday

No connection. The train would be six hours
late, it was announced, and that Maundy Thursday
I sat for six hours in the airless dark
of the waiting room of Kocsárd's tiny station.
My soul was heavy and my body broken –
I felt like one who, on a secret journey,
sets out in darkness, summoned by the stars
on fateful earth, braving yet fleeing doom;
whose nerves are so alert that he can sense
enemies, far off, tracking him by stealth.
Outside the window engines rumbled by
and dense smoke like the wing of a huge bat
brushed my face. I felt dull horror, gripped
by a deep bestial fear. I looked around:
it would have been so good to speak a little
to close friends, a few words to men you trust,
but there was only damp night, dark and chill,
Peter was now asleep, and James and John
asleep, and Matthew, all of them asleep...
Thick beads of cold sweat broke out on my brow
and then streamed down over my crumpled face.

[CW/GG]

A Confession

Where I live is like an island.
Each day what can I do
but kneel – preoccupied
by nothing except you?
It may be the sun cools,
it may be the moon will fall,
this resonant otherworld
dissolves me, absorbs me whole.

It has sweet fragrances,
the light has its own tricks,
the laws governing it
are happy as they are strict.
What elsewhere would be measured
by the tick of a small clock
here by the steady throbbing
in your breast is marked;
you speak and each soft word
that, dreamily, you yield
becomes a silver flower
set in a blue field;
and your sigh is the wind
stirring in my hair,
and your face has the moon's glow,
and your face has the sun's glare.

[CW/GG]

Last Year's Love

A memory that glitters,
though sometimes too it glares
at my pallid face, as I look
back into past years.
It was bright as a star is bright,
like fire it gave off heat,
also as white as snow
and, like honey, sweet.

I see its gleam at times
but the torment has now ceased;
it's a cool, friendly hand –
I feel its light caress.
It has fallen like a star,
it has gone out like fire,
it's melted as snow melts
and the sweetness has turned sour.

[CW/GG]

The Poem of Darkness

Once more, the vigil season!
Broad pen-strokes on my sheet look grim.
Night's rust-juice floods the gardens,
by six full to the brim.
Damp oozes from the mouldering trees,
you muse on how much time
you've left. Your foot stops dead, in fear
of stumbling into a tomb...
But tell me: have you ever let
a snow-white sugar-cube soak up
dark liquid, dipped in the bitter night
of coffee in its cup?
Or watched how the dense liquid,
so surely, so insidiously,
will seep up through the white cube's
pure, crystalline body?
Just so the night seeps into you,
slowly rising, the smells
of night and of the grave all through
your veins, fibres, cells,
until one dank brown evening,
so steeped in it, you melt and sink –
to sweeten, for some unknown god,
his dark and bitter drink.

[CW/GG]

MIKLÓS RADNÓTI

A Mountain Garden

Summer has fallen asleep, it drones, and a grey veil
  Is drawn across the bright face of the day;
  A shadow vaults a bush, so my dog growls,
  His hackles bristling, and then runs away.

Shedding its petals one by one, a late flower stands
  Naked and half-alive; I hear the sound
  Of a withered apricot-bough crack overhead
  To sink of its own weight slowly to the ground.

O, and the garden too prepares for sleep, its fruit
  Proffered to the heavy season of the dead.
  It is getting dark. Late too, a golden bee
  Is flying a death-circle around my head.

And as for you, young man, what mode of death awaits you?
  Will a shot hum like a beetle toward your heart,
  Or a loud bomb rend the earth so that your body
  Falls limb from limb, your young flesh torn apart?

In sleep the garden breathes; I question it in vain;
  Though still unanswered I repeat it all.
  The noonday sun still flows in the ripe fruit
  Touched by the twilight chill of the dew fall.

Istenhegy (a Buda mountain), 1936

[CW/GG]

The First Eclogue

> *'Quippe ubi fas versum atque nefas: tot bella per orbem,*
> *Tam multae scelerum facies...'*
>   VIRGIL, *Georgics* I, 505-06

Shepherd:

It is long since we last met here; did the song of the thrushes call
        you?

Poet:

I'm listening to the woods: there is such a din now spring's here!

Shepherd:

This isn't spring – the sky wants to fool us – just look at this
        puddle:
Now it is smiling meekly, but at night when the frost congeals it
It'll bare its teeth! This is April – a fool's month to believe in:
Those little tulips there have been nipped in the bud by frost.
Why sad? Won't you sit down here on this stone beside me?

Poet:

It's not that I'm sad; I have grown used to this terrible world
So far, that sometimes I am not hurt by it – merely disgusted.

Shepherd:

What I heard is now certain: amid corpses stiff with blood,
On the ridges of the wild Pyrenees, red-hot cannon wrangle,
And bears, it is said, join with the soldiers as they flee;
In flocks, with knotted bundles, flee old folk, women and children,
Throwing themselves on the ground as Death starts circling above,
And there are so many lying dead, they are left there – no one
        removes them.
I think you knew Federico – did he escape, ah tell me!

Poet:

He did not flee. Two years ago he was killed in Granada.

Shepherd:

García Lorca is dead! And you are the first to tell me!
The news of war travels so very fast, and yet poets
Just disappear like that! Did Europe not mourn his death?

Poet:
It was not even noticed. At best only the wind, that gropes
Through the pyre's ashes, will find some broken line to remember.
This much is left, no more, to the curious who come after us.

Shepherd:
He did not flee, he died. But then where can a poet escape?
Nor did our loved Attila József flee, but said *no*
To the present State; yet tell me, who mourns him now he has fallen?
How do you live? Can your words still find an echo in these times?

Poet:
While cannon boom? Among smouldering ruins, deserted villages?
Still, I keep on writing and live in this frenzied world
As that oak over there: it knows it will be cut down and already
Is marked with a white cross, showing that there, tomorrow,
The woodcutter begins. Yet, as it waits, it puts forth a new leaf.
You are fortunate here: it's so still – few wolves come this way,
And as it is months since your master was last here, you can often
Forget that the flock you tend belongs to somebody else.
God bless you; time I get home, old night will have fallen upon me;
The butterfly dusk is fluttering, its wings shedding silver sift.

1938

[CW/GG]

The Second Eclogue

Pilot:
We came so far last night; I almost laughed with fury,
fighters like swarms of bees buzzed in the upper story:
a hot defence, good shooting – they'd beaten out our brains,
till the horizon filled up with new swarms of our planes
they almost mopped the floor with us, swatted us from the sky,
but see, I'm here again! Tomorrow by and by
Europe will know I'm coming, and trembling hide away...
Enough of this! Friend, did you write since yesterday?

Poet:
Write – what else could I do? The poet writes, the cat
will mew, dog howl and have his day, the fish coquett-
ishly set out its eggs. Of everything I write,
so you'll know how I live – you, even, in your height –
when through the blasted houses slumping in toppled rows
the sick light of the bloodshot moon staggers as it goes,
and public squares all quaking rear upward with the shock,
so that the earth is gagging, the sky itself must choke,
and still the waves of planes come over and are gone,
and then return – insanity! – to strafe the shattered town.
Write – what else can I do? If you but knew the peril
of a poem, a line however whimsical
or delicate – there's courage in this too, the poet
writes, the poor dog howls, the little fish, the cat –
and so on...what do you know? Nothing! all you hear
is the machine, you're deaf with it, it's what you are,
your friend, your other nature: this you can't deny.
What do you think about, above us in the sky?

Pilot:
You'll laugh. I'm terrified up here. Eyes closed, I miss
just lying about in bed, I miss my sweetheart's kiss,
or else I hum about it softly through my teeth
above the vaporous hell's kitchen there beneath.
Up here I would be down. Down there I want to fly.
No place upon the earth is fit for such as I.
I am indeed condemned to love a dead machine,
for we have ached to the same beat where we have been...
But you know this, and you will write my secret down,
that I, who am destroyer, lived once as a man,
I who am an exile between the earth and sky...
Ah, who could know or write the mystery of I?
Will you?

Poet:
    If I and those I write for do not die.

27 April 1941

[ZsO/FT]

Foaming Sky

The moon bobs on the sky's foam;
I wonder at being alive tonight.
Assiduous Death keeps searching our dark time
And those he finds are all unearthly white.

Sometimes the year looks back, lets out a scream,
Looks back, then passes out appalled.
Again what a grim autumn's crouched behind me
And what a winter, numbed by pain and dulled!

The forest bled and, in the cycle
Of time, each hour would shed its blood.
The wind scrawled numbers, vast and dark,
On the snow drifts in the wood.

I have come to see both that and this;
I feel how heavily air weighs on the earth;
A warm silence, alive with rustling noises,
Envelops me – as before birth.

I stop under a tree whose leaves
Seethe with anger. Its branches creak –
One reaches down: to grasp my throat?
I am no coward, nor am I weak,

But tired. I hold my tongue. The branch
Gropes through my hair in silence, fearfully.
I know one ought to forget, but I
Never forget a single memory.

The moon founders in foam; across the sky
A dark-green track of poison has been driven.
I stand and roll myself a cigarette,
Slowly, carefully. I am living.

8 June 1940

[CW/GG]

Autumn Begins Restlessly...

The sun upsurges restlessly, being lapped
By fire-fringed, iron-grey flags;
Its vapours stream down, and the floating light
Bites into lowering fogs.

The clouds are ruffled, the smooth pane of the sky
Is rippled by wind, the blue flies away.
The low flight of a swallow preparing to leave
Describes a screaming 'e' or 'a'.

Autumn begins restlessly: the rust
On dying leaves sways up and down
And the sky's breath is cool.
The sky gives off no warmth – nothing but smoke;
The sun no more than sighs today, and feebly.

A lizard scuttles on the great graveyard wall;
Autumn's ravenous wasps,
All gorging on flesh, are buzzing rabidly.

Men, on the banked earth
Of trenches, sit and stare
At the deep fires of death;
The smell of heavy leaf-mould floats on the air.

Flame flies above the road –
Half-light, half-blood, it flares on the coming dark.
Brown leaves, burning in the wind,
Flutter, spark.

And clustered grapes weigh on the vine, the vine-shoots
        wither;
Drily the stems of yellow flowers
Crackle, and seeds fall to the ground.

The meadow is swimming in the evening mist;
At length, the wild clattering sound
Of distant carts shakes from the trees
The few leaves that persist.

The landscape falls asleep;
Death, lovely in his white glide,
Flies down on the countryside;
The sky cradles the garden.
Look: in your hair's an autumn leaf that's golden;
For above you, branches weep.

Ah, but your flame must rise above death and autumn,
And raise me, love, along with you;
Let the wise thing be to love me today –
Be wise and kiss me, hungry for dreams too.

Jóyfully love me, do not leave me, fall
With me into the dark sky sleep creates.
Let's sleep. Out there, the thrush is well asleep;
The walnut, falling on fallen leaves piled deep,
Makes no harsh sound. And reason disintegrates.

[CW/GG]

Neither Memory Nor Magic

A great but hidden anger clung in my heart before,
like seeds as brown as negroes within the apple-core;
I knew an angel watched me, a great sword in his hand,
to care, protect and follow me in danger's shadow-land.

But he – who has awoken, a ghost in that brutal dawn,
when everything's in ruins, and he must be up and gone,
his body almost naked, his few things left behind,
whose lovely lightstep heart must now learn to find
the cryptic musing humbleness of an older man –
rebels against things other than he did when he was free,
strives toward the future, the glow of liberty.
I never owned possessions and now I never shall.
Think for a moment: life's so rich and prodigal;
I bear no anger in my heart, would not avenge the wrong;

always the world rebuilds; though they forbid my song,
in the new wall's foundations my word will sing and be;
now it's for me to live out what there's left to me,
and I will not look back now, for neither memory
nor magic will protect me from these omens in the sky.
Turn from me when you see me, friend, throw up your hands.
Where once an angel with a sword stood guard,
now, perhaps, no one stands.

30 April 1944

[ZsO/FT]

Letter to My Wife

Deep down there, worlds dumb and silent lie:
The silence howling in my ears, I cry
But no one here can answer me in far
Serbia that, stunned, crumpled into war;
And you are far off. Twined around my dreams
Is your voice – which, by day, my heart reclaims.
So I am silent; cool to the touch and proud,
The many ferns around me hum aloud.

When I can see you once again – who were
Lovely as light, lovely as shadow, sure
And grave as a psalm is – I do not know;
Were I blind and dumb, I'd find you even so.
My mind projects you: in landscape you hide
But flash upon my eyes from deep inside.
You are but a dream again now, who were real;
My adolescence – I fall back down that well

And question you 'Do you love me?' jealously,
And hope again that one day you will be
(When I have reached my prime of youth) my wife;
I fall back on the road of conscious life
Then, for I know you are. My wife and friend.

But far off. Three cruel frontiers intervened.
Slowly it's autumn. Will that too leave me here?
The memory of our kisses grows more clear;

I once believed in miracles – now though
I forget their dates...Above me bombers go...
I was just admiring your eyes' blue in the sky,
But clouds came and a plane up there flew by
With bombs longing to fall. A prisoner,
I live despite them. All I have hopes for
I've thought out, yet I'll find my way to you,
For I have walked the soul's full length for you –

And the roads of all these lands; through scarlet ash
I'll charm my way if need be, through the crash
Of worlds on fire – and yet I shall get back.
If need be, I'll be tough as a tree's bark;
And the calm that hardened men have, who each hour
Know danger, stress, – a calm worth guns and power –
Soothes me and, like a cool wave of the sea,
Sobering, 'two-times-two' breaks over me.

Lager Heideman,
August–September 1944

[CW/GG]

The Eighth Eclogue

Poet:
Hail! You endure well this rugged mountain walk,
Fine old man; is it that wings lift you or enemies hunt you?
Wings bear you, passion drives you, lightning flares in your eyes.
Hail, venerable elder! Now I perceive you are one of
The ireful prophets of old – but, tell me, which of their number?

Prophet:
Which am I? I am Nahum the Elkoshite. It was I
Who thundered against the concupiscent city of Nineveh, I
Who declaimed the Word of the Lord, his brimming vessel of
          anger!

Poet:
I know your ancient fury; your writings have been preserved.

Prophet:
They have. But now, more than of old, sin multiplies,
Yet, even now, there is no one who knows what the Lord's end is.
For the Lord said he would cause the abundant rivers to dry up,
Bashan to languish, and Carmel, and Lebanon's flower to wither,
The mountains would quake, and everything be consumed in fire.
And all this befell.

Poet:
                    Whole nations scramble to the slaughter,
And the soul of Man is stripped bare, even as Nineveh.
What use had admonitions? And the savage, ravening locusts
In their green clouds, what effect? Of all beasts, Man is the basest!
Here, tiny babes are dashed against walls and, over there,
The church tower is a torch, the house an oven roasting
Its own people. Whole factories fly up in their smoke.
The street runs mad with people on fire, then swoons with a wail,
The vast bomb-bays disgorge, the great clamps loose their burdens,
And shrivelled, like a herd's dung on a pasture, the dead lie
Spattering city squares: everything, once again,
Has happened as you foretold. Tell me, what brings you back
To earth from ancient cloud-swirl?

Prophet:
                    Wrath: that Man, as ever,
Is an orphan again among the hosts of the seeming-human,
The heathen. And I wish again to see the strongholds of sin
Fall – wish to bear witness for the ages yet to come.

Poet:
You have already done so. And the Lord spoke through you long
          ago:
Cried woe to the fortress filled with the spoils of war – with bastions

Built of corpses! But tell me, can it be so that fury
Has survived in you these millennia – with divine, unquenchable
     blaze?

Prophet:
There was a time when the Lord touched my unclean lips
As he did the sage Isaiah's. With his ember hovering over me
God probed my heart. The coal was a live coal and red-hot –
An angel held it with tongs and, 'Look, here am I: let me
Also be called upon to preach thy Word,' I cried after him.
And once a man has been sent by the Lord, he has no age,
He has no peace. That coal, angelic, burns on in his lips.
And what is a thousand years to the Lord? A mayfly time!

Poet:
How young you are, father! I envy you. What is my own brief
     time
To your awesome age? Even these few fleeting moments
Are wearing me down – like a round stone in a wild stream.

Prophet:
So you may think. But I know your new poems. Wrath nurtures
     you.
The poet's wrath, much like the prophet's, is food and drink
To the people. Whoever would may live on it until
The coming of the Kingdom that young disciple promised,
The young Rabbi whose life fulfilled our words and the Law.
Come with me to preach that already the hour is at hand,
The Kingdom about to be born. 'What,' I asked before,
'Is the Lord's end?' Lo, it is that Kingdom. Come let us go:
Gather the people together. Bring your wife. Cut staffs.
For the wanderer, staffs are good companions. Look, give me that
     one –
There: let me have that one: I like the gnarled ones better.

Lager Heideman,
23 August 1944

[CW/GG]

À la Recherche...

You too, past gentle evenings, are being refined into memory!
Bright table, once adorned by poets and their young women,
Where in the mud of the past, now, do you slide away to?
Where is the night when friends, sparkling with wit and gusto,
Still drank their fine hock gaily from bright-eyed slender glasses?

Lines of poetry swam around in the lamplight, brilliant
Green adjectives swayed on the metre's foaming crest and
Those who are dead now were living, the prisoners still home,
          and all of
Those dear friends who are missing, the long-ago-fallen, wrote
          poems.
Their hearts are under the soil of Flanders, Ukraine and Iberia.

There were men of a kind who gritted their teeth, ran into gunfire
And fought – only because they could do nothing against it,
And while, sheltered by the filthy night, the company
Slept restlessly round them, they'd be thinking of rooms they had
          lived in –
Islands and caves to them inside this hostile order.

There were places they travelled to in tight-sealed cattle wagons;
They had to stand, unarmed and freezing, in the minefields.
There was also a place they went to, guns in their hands and willing,
Without a word: they saw their own cause in that struggle.
And now the angel of freedom guards their deep dream nightly.

There were places...No matter. Where are the wise, wine-drinking
          parties?
Their call-up papers flew to them, fragmentary poems multiplied,
And wrinkles multiplied, too, around the lips and under
The eyes of young women with lovely smiles: girls who in bearing
Were sylph-like grew heavy during the silent years of the war-time.

Where is the night, the bar, the table under the lime-trees?
And those still alive, where are they – those herded into the battle?
My hand still clasps their hands, my heart still hears their voices;
I recall their works – I perceive the stature of their torsos
Which appear to me, silent prisoner, on the wailing heights of
          Serbia.

Where is that night? That night will never more come back to us,
For whatever has passed on, death alters its perspectives.
They sit down at the table, they hide in the smiles of women,
And shall sip wine from our glasses: they who now, unburied,
Sleep in faraway forests, sleep in distant pastures.

Lager Heideman,
17 August 1944

[CW/GG]

Forced March

A fool he is who, collapsed,   rises and walks again,
Ankles and knees moving   alone, like wandering pain,
Yet he, as if wings uplifted him,   sets out on his way,
And in vain the ditch calls him   back, who dare not stay.
And if asked why not, he might answer   – without leaving his
          path –
That his wife was awaiting him,   and a saner, more beautiful death.
Poor fool! He's out of his mind: now, for a long time,
Only scorched winds have whirled   over the houses at home,
The wall has been laid low,   the plum-tree is broken there,
The night of our native hearth   flutters, thick with fear.
O if only I could believe   that everything of worth
Were not just in my heart –   that I still had a home on earth;
If only I had! As before,   jam made fresh from the plum
Would cool on the old verandah,   in peace the bee would hum,
And an end-of-summer stillness   would bask in the drowsy garden,
Naked among the leaves   would sway the fruit trees' burden,
And She would be waiting, blonde   against the russet hedgerow,
As the slow morning painted slow   shadow over shadow, –
Could it perhaps still be?   The moon tonight's so round!
Don't leave me friend, shout at me: I'll get up off the ground!

15 September 1944

[CW/GG]

GYÖRGY FALUDY

Western Australia

This stamp has been troubling my eyes for two long days;
it shows a swimming swan, a skipper of smooth waters;
I knew it in my boyhood, one of the old issues,
WESTERN AUSTRALIA blocked out in black letters.

Australia in that century past: a scene
of bearded men striding jerkily on their way
beside mud-covered wagons and strong yoked oxen,
gripping in their tanned fists the old long pipes of clay.

Light falls upon the clearing, an axe of silver;
on the shore of the lake the silent patient house
seems undersea, smoke like the chain of an anchor
twisting and soaring up to a fleet of stars.

Women in violet taffeta; on hills of breasts,
like the spokes of a wheel, their infants are turning.
Sometimes one gazes at herself in a glass
with a crude cast-iron frame; they know no aging.

Newspapers reach them seldom; History is slow
moving; they know nothing of Bismarck or Kruger
till at last the first road appears, white as snow,
and, in a green jacket, the telegraph operator.

The sandstorm of sheep outside grows more dense each day;
at evening, on the kitchen stoves, stews bubble;
a pocket torch – a marvel – arrives from Adelaide,
for the wife a muff, for the son a water pistol.

Sometimes they get together. Holidays are special.
In a smoky inn with an oil lamp hung on a chain
in voices thunderous enough to block out exile's
tears, they toast Victoria, their white-haired queen.

At dusk old couples sit on benches in the garden;
the day's last light on the lake lies flat, serene,
as the great swan arrives, glides, hardly moving,
as peaceful happy and proud as these lives have been.

Here I stop, startled, and realise what I'm doing,
ashamed that only two short years of this prison,
some times of terror, some kicking and some beating,
have sufficed to send me seeking that marvellous swan,

and I, like a Sleeping Beauty still awaiting
my country's awakening kiss, have forgotten Faith,
Fame, Ethics – twined on a stick by my day-dreaming
have become a pioneer on foreign earth,

a subject of Queen Victoria, who's long since dead,
a happy corpse myself, no more a live pariah,
and have asked your dusty glory to bless my forehead
your powdery, good, free soil, Western Australia.

'Not so!' I cry, and, smiling, stand up, still bloody
from the latest kicks and beatings, and swear, 'Instead,
though jailed and shackled, I will fight this tyranny,
give it no peace from my rhymes, not even when dead,

beginning again and again after every failure,
until my country is beautiful, new, and free;
if ever I should leave it will be for Australia
and I will bring that black swan home with me.'

Punishment cell, Recsk, 1952

[RS]

Swedish Rococo

The sleigh is waiting here outside
the house, and they jump up together,
Ulla from the left-hand side,
Karl Michael from the other.

The pony moves into a canter;
snow crunches as the sleigh runs on,
and the smooth ice of Lake Malar
is popping like Dom Perignon.

The beau looks at his lovely belle
and tells himself, 'This is my Ulla,
today as sweet as caramel,
tomorrow a meringue cadaver.'

The belle looks at her handsome beau:
'My Bellman who makes pretty poems!
The roof may fall on him tomorrow,
but poets are never stilled by tombs.'

They whistle duets, minuets.
The roof of the lake-shore hotel
is wooden, pointed, pierced with frets
and Royalty have liked it well.

They disembark and Bellman places
a swollen nosebag on the pony
who does not eat a grain, but glances
slyly at the lovely lady.

In the hotel the air is thick
with smoke and smells of ham and beans.
Predictably, the girl is quick
to find the stairs, and up she runs.

Mine host lifts up a glass to Bellman,
toasting him in aquavit,
imploring him for everyone
to join the fellowship of wit.

The company, lovers of Voltaire,
are keen for intellectual chat,
but butterflies of poets don't care
to waste their wingbeats upon that.

He very much prefers to seize
a vintage bottle from the Beaune
and cookies flavoured with anise,
most excellent when hard as stone.

The mansard room is filled with fragrance
and heated more than laws permit.
The toilet boasts Gustav Adolphus,
engraved in copper, ruling it.

Ulla is waiting on the bed,
naked as on her natal day –
though now, some twenty years ahead,
more practised in the ways to play.

She parts her thighs, lifts up her knees,
but, being still a lady and
rococo, is ashamed to please
and hides her face between her hands.

Bellman has put down the dish.
She is the loveliest of girls.
He tenderly begins to kiss
her fairest and most private curls

and finds: 'A wire brush, by thunder!
A hedgehog could be hardly worse.
And yet she's loving it. I wonder
who taught her to be thus perverse.'

While Ulla: 'How I do dislike
these tickling primitive sensations!
Still, it is for his poetry's sake.
My name will live for generations.'

Now Bellman, stepping to the window,
closes the shutters, which are shaking.
The sunlight scatters on the snow
bright chips like some woodworker's shavings.

The pony at the gate is stamping
and staring up. He does not eat,
and, being innocent of clothing,
is all too visibly in heat.

The pony's eyes engage the poet's
and there's a flash of understanding.
'Just look at him, the randy beast!
He's jealous – may the Devil damn him!'

High up, the slatted shutters close;
down in the snow the pony neighs,
and, lifting up his velvet nose,
gives such a sudden sneeze he sprays
gold showers of oats into the breeze.

Stockholm, 1962

[RS]

Sonnet Eighty-Five

At Heathrow, Andrew waits to drive us to Brighton.
Above our heads the aeroplanes are shrieking
and by the road old farmhouses are abandoned
and there's a roofless pub. I stare, say nothing.

Between the windowless houses no hint of people,
far off sirens wail and dry winds blow
dust and powdered concrete; instead of apples,
in the boughs of a dead tree squats a crow.

The car rolls smoothly onward. There is no need
for any kind of comment. We exchange
quick glances, then look down, relieved that greed
had robbed our fellow mortals of the brain

to sense that we exist one step before
the world's collapse, or maybe one step after.

Brighton, 1978

[RS]

In the Reading Room of the British Museum

Beside me sits an aged woman in
a housecoat, wearing dirty tennis-shoes
(it's winter now) and shabby woollen stockings,
all neatly tied with string and safety-pins.
At lunch time as I eat roast beef I watch
her count out six-pence for a mug of tea
then choose a fag-end from a tin and smoke.
She's spent the morning reading cuneiform,
a codex without notes, without translation.

At quarter to nine each morning I wait
beneath the columns for the doors to open.
The regulars are there already, come
on foot from dreary rooms in Bloomsbury.
That's where they eat and live on God knows what:
don't ask, because for once that's not the question.
The aged woman, and the long-haired boy
who seeks the Cathari in Provençal
for their magnificence, the red-faced man
who's wrestled fifty years with Abelard.
Gradually I've come to recognise them all.

These are my people though I'm from a land
where no one tolerates a man who tries
to save himself. I envy them and feel
ashamed: they study but they don't take notes
as I do, scribbling here, my publisher's
pathetic cheque already in the bank.
They are my tribe, a tribe condemned to death.
Every day's their holiday, and Sundays
they sit alone amidst a paradise
of renaissances, small beacons in a world
where renaissances occur in books alone.

An unknown god has been their host on earth
and spread a blue Sarouk beneath their feet;
they've built a crystal cloister for themselves
where factory whistles never sound, and money
never talks – where silence hovers over worth.

And one day on their deathbeds they'll sit up
and know in silence what a billion men
will never know: that, living, they were alive.

London, 1967

[EJ]

ISTVÁN VAS

Gods

Gods, arraigned so often and so often!

You beasts and monsters, rivers some, and stars,
Dog-headed ones and hundred-nippled ones,
Some marine, some subterrene, some nurtured
On the nursery-floors of underworlds, fen-dwellers,
Attendants of the departed, corpse-devourers,
And totems come of even older strains
Of noble stock, rearing up, stone-faced spirits,
Mounded a-tilt, tent-like, Inferno peacocks,

Never have I prostrated myself before you,
Never in your name gone through a hocus-pocus,
And yet I know you exist, I recognise you
In any form, in the fraudulent arguments
Of an allegedly science-based aesthetics,
In the peristaltic paroxysms of visions,
A consciously sombre rhetoric's sparse emissions,
Or in the ambiguously apathetic
Smile picked up unawares from a young physique,
I know you exist, and it may be, sooner or later,
You will contrive to get me in your clutches.

And yet perhaps – at heart this is what I hope for –
I have succeeded in slipping out of your grasp,
And you can whistle for me, unwieldy
Mask-wearers, prodigies tricked out hooligan-fashion
And you, the light-bearers, archers, gazers at the sun,
You with the brains of fire, strainers of nerves,

Wearers of helms, shield-wielders, bearers of
Victory on the helm, on the shield the monster's head
Borne to the light, killers of dragons, good swordsmen,
The sunlight-bodied, the from-the-seas-emerging
From among the monsters to unprecedented pleasures,
The beautiful, the illuminations, the
Descenders to hell, overcomers of hell's forces,
Pilfering plunderers of the underworlds,

You have I never professed in hymns nor in
The covertly moustached and self-effacing
Erudite smile of a specialised monograph;
But you have I had with me in the combat.
How often was the shield not held before me, hiding
How often has your spear not thrust for me!
How often have you not sent me the good enveloping mist!
When I was imperilled, and when I fled, you were with me,
When I invented, when I overcame,
And you have been with me in many and many a bed.
Vigour-enduers you, and beauty-pursuers,
You of the bright hearts, you whom I have found,
Surely you know I am yours, and you will surely
Send me down the envoy, the attendant,
The god of poets and of thieves and secrets,
Him, the father of all stratagems,
To be my convoy on my slippery road,
To essay, when I must come to changing over
From form to form, his best wiles for my good,
When I shall step from the one into the other?

[DD]

Pest Elegy

Remarkable city: mud slopping filth. February strives
To cover the purple of mourning with slush, and a hard rain drives
The rubbish before it, the rubbish which thickens and thrives.

Soot settles, blackening turrets of snow: skeletal, bloody,
The city is shivering in puddles, both of us muddy,
Emerging together: the city is one with my own frozen body.

Fog swathes the Ring Road; a thin ersatz gauze serves for a binding,
Above the hulks of the Royal and Emke the smoke has stopped
        winding,
Through teetering gaps new lights in the New York are pulsing
        and blinding.

A tortured frivolity flickers, struggles once more to its feet,
And clings to the city a murderous climate failed to defeat,
Refusing to flounder in mortar or drown in the swill of the street.

Ten o'clock. Life's neons are blinking. Soon they will stop.
Despair is a drunkard who lurches and heaves in the slop.
A thin throbbing of motors at night: Pest hunched for the drop.

What voices have rung down these streets, or flew to address
Impossible hopes but whistled out nevertheless
The youthful and brilliant logic of ultimate cleanliness!

The light in our eyes, in our mutual glances, remembers the glow –
We remember it all, the lot, my poor friends, is it not so?
The irregular beat in the stone heart of town gives our hearts the go.

Though the stone heart of town keeps on missing, its beats never
          die.
But even if fate should leave not a stone standing, time would
          raise high
The stack of her walls once again, with its right of reply.

For it's neither the stone, nor the beam, nor the wall, nor any
          such quiddity;
Demolish the fabric a hundred times over, there still stands a city:
She has purchased from Death itself her share of eternity.

The city has purchased herself and redeemed me as well:
My guilt floats in gutters and ditches, in winter's apparel.
The great absolution is here, in the present, and I can feel hell

Slip from my heart with the sorrow that's stamped and suffered
          alone:
Redeeming herself, the city redeems me as one of her own.
Forgiveness, unhoped for, glows from her body, from bruised
          flesh and bone.

The lights are all out now but faith dawns through faint foggy
          weather.
The record remains, entered by somebody, somehow, wherever:
I lived here, nor wanted any place else. Not then and not ever.

[GSz]

The Invisible Element

To that invisible element which claimed
A part in our becoming fact not fiction,
Which turned what knowledge and desire had framed
Against itself in direct contradiction –

What could you possibly say? That our schemes ripen
To performance, that thoughts petrify
To form? The bonds of contemplation tighten
From cradle to the grave, and so we die.

At what point did the fatal germ infect
The process of becoming with its lies?
Or was it bred within the intellect?
We hoped for more? No, this was no surprise.

What do you know? If you were still alive
What could you say? Or were you wrong as well?
No answer. Yet the very germs which thrive
Are sweeter than grace although they give us hell.

[GSz]

Rhapsody in an Autumn Garden

Patches of damp invade your garden of light.
The sun rises late, remains a few short hours,
Frosts blacken and bite
Your dahlias, sunflowers,
Late autumn fires the petals of helianthus
Which gasp for the sun – but soon run out of time.
Their mortality illuminates and haunts us –
We do not share it with their kind.

The little cherry tree blushes – but how would it be
If the clouds suddenly burst (as well they might)?
Red leaves are lovelier when spinning free
Before damp wind in charismatic flight.
Already a deep natural instinct waits
On the punishment of stiff November showers:
Here at least the beautiful defeats
More ruinous powers.

I think of us – our hearts and guts and all.
I have no fear, for you or me, of death.
But why reach winter, should it be possible,
Brimming with self-disgust at every breath.
In beauty leaves and flowers pass away –
But those who grasp at stars and lose their thread,
What can they do when winter bars their way
With earthly loathsomeness and dread?

Frozen dahlias, roses: our garden revives
And rises in full beauty though destroyed.
Now we'll see what we have gained, what thrives
Beyond skin, organ, gut and void.
It's autumn yet so fight with a will,
Defend yourself and earn remission
Until the victorious knowledge in the cell
Embarks on its final expedition.

In ten thousand years has there ever been
A beauty that has not been ours?
Do ordinary leaves and flowers
Store their light for the winter unseen?
There's nothing to be ashamed of:
There's more of beauty even in our foul
Decline, than in all the glittering stuff
Of flowers or of fowl.

Why else accumulate beauty from day to day
So prudently, what is it for
If not so that even in life's final struggle there may
Be beauty in store?
The masters, our ancestors, were not trifling when they
Created noble, lovely monuments:
They meant them for your last line of defence
In our wars against the forces of decay.

What do the flowers or vegetation know?
Imperious rockets, pursue your explosive trajectories!
Ours are beauties not of the earth: they grow
Down human centuries.
And always there's you and I – on Mars
Or the moon or wherever, who can tell,
Until we discover such magic formulas
We cannot rest nor sleep too well.

And time will yield you energies whose burning brand
Will set alight new constellations.
What's terrible now will turn to consolation,
And you will see and I will understand,
Your suffering reveal a pattern
More joyful, lovely, with greater powers:
And in your smile will open those long forgotten
Dahlias, sunflowers.

[GSz]

Romanus Sum

Romanus sum – and I held my hand in fire;
Through twenty years it has burnt me to the bone.
I played the part of Mucius Scaevola
Before what would, though yet unborn, be Rome.

And suddenly it was here. All that the past
Has spewed ferments between its malformed walls.
Rome has not yet been built but in its place,
Bloated with lies, a new Byzantium swells.

And the crucifix is debased to a gilded bauble
And the flames of Pentecost lap a martyr's stake.
It was such a waste to have burnt one's living flesh
For a stillborn City's sake.

c. 1952

[CW/GG]

Upon a Drawing

These feet and hands, two pelvises, this movement
Is unmistakeable. But who was it had
Such a narrow face? Who between mouth and brow
Such a long, narrow cavity? This skull, balding,
Yes, this one I know – but who looks through these eyes?
This one, and that one. They are making love –
Not two, but many of them. Those dead
Lovers and wives move in their intimate
Movement. In these lines men and women,
Irreconcilable once, now come together.
What lines! What an embrace!
This coitus of line that is poured in white across
A background of black, how richly laden it is,
Rich in its purity, pure too in its lust!
Such lust is available only to those who already
Are no more, who exist in these lines alone, hidden
In this embrace. In this framework, translucent, yet
Ingeniously solid. And in all the signs of life
Of this exclusive multitude, only they, only they
Can be named, these two. You and I, you and I.

(On a drawing by the poet's wife, Piroska Szántó)

[CW/GG]

SÁNDOR WEÖRES

The Colonnade of Teeth

1

The Colonnade of Teeth, where you have entered,
red marble hall: your mouth,
white marble columns: your teeth,
and the scarlet carpet you step on: your tongue.

2

You can look out of any window of time
and catch sight of still another face of God.
Lean out of the time of sedge and warblers:
God caresses.
Lean out of the time of Moses and Elijah:
God haggles.
Lean out of the time of the Cross:
God's face is all blood, like Veronica's napkin.
Lean out of your own time:
God is old, bent over a book.

3

Head downwards, like Peter on his cross,
man hangs in the blue sky with flaring hair
and the earth trundles over the soles of his feet.
The one who sees
has sleepless eyes he cannot take from man.

4

No sugar left for the child:
he stuffs himself with hen-droppings and finds what's sweet.
Every clod: lightless star!
Every worm: wingless cherub!

5

If you make hell, plunge to the bottom:
heaven's in sight there. Everything circles round.

6

Man lays down easy roads.
The wild beast stamps a forest track.
And look at the tree: depth and height raying from it to every
        compass-point;
itself a road, to everywhere!

7

Once you emerge from the glitter of the last two columns
the cupola your hair skims is then infinity,
and a swirl of rose-leaves throws you down,
and all that lies below, your bridal bed: the whole world –
Here you can declare:
'My God, I don't believe in you!'
And the storm of rose-leaves will smile:
'But I believe in you: are you satisfied?'

[EM]

De Profundis

Whatever my origin, driven out into the earth,
my clothes will always carry the sheepfold stench
    of things here below.
This is the place where God's every plant and beast
pullulates through its appalling feast,
    chewing its neighbours raw.

I confess it was not good I expected to find,
but such a freight of misery was far from my mind:
    a son of a different star,
if he had even one minute's taste of our pain,
plunged into molten ore with sparks like rain,
    would soon be steam and air.

We swing from keen to glum, from gloom to joy,
up and down, up and down in our seesaw,
    swung without a say,
like someone forced by torturers to watch
a strobe of light and dark until they hatch
    his madness in that way.

Any reason in this world is a poor by-blow of Reason,
scrabbling at the mere shell of things, seizing
    nothing near the bone.
Half-asleep in half-darkness we slump,
wrestling through our fray in the deep swamp,
    our prison and our home:

for what are we but cannibals of each other,
buying our own life with the death of a brother:
    earth's law, earth's fee.
What are brothers but stone, tree, beast, man,
I eat my brother with gut-slithering pain,
    and my brother eats me.

An alley cat laps a young chick's blood:
one twists in death, one fights for food:
    I suffer both the same.
Rocks are crushed, earth's flesh punctured, cut:
neither stone nor earth knows any hurt,
    but I have the pain.

When anything is killed, I am killed,
the earth with all its miseries and ills
    gapes me its jaws.
A fly hits a flame: I'm writhing there,
I'm dying a thousand times every hour
    and without a pause.

Split the veil into the next existence,
and I shall still look shivering down the vistas
    and pits of this world.
There would be no assuaging even in heaven:
God's own light will build no haven,
    nor my lament grow cold.

[EM]

Queen Tatavane

O my winged ancestors!
Green branch and dry twig you gave me
for my two empires, to plant one and to lash one.
I am small as a weasel, pure as the eastern Moon,
light-ankled as a gazelle, but not poised for flight –
my heart lies open to you, to every silent suggestion.

The Elephantstar took my fifteenth year,
the Dragonstar brought this, the sixteenth.
I am allowed three husbands by ancestral decree
and seven lovers beneath the holy jasmine-leaves.

Not for me to escape with girl-friends to the fields,
for happy laughter, goats to milk, fresh milk to drink,
instead I sit on the throne in your light, year after year,
an ebony idol with the world's weight on my neck.

Negro caravans, Arab ships are my traffic and merchandise,
I pay well, though I see most as polecats and monkeys,
but even the sky rains on unchosen ground, seeds burst unchosen.
I survey the naked hosts lost in their prison,
all of them I love as if they were my children,
punishing them with the rod and if need be by the sword,
and though my heart should bleed my looks are frozen.

Wake up, my fathers and mothers! Leave the ash-filled urn,
help me while the mists crawl;
your dark little daughter pleads with you as the last queen,
waiting among the garlands of the cedar-hall.

My seat among stone lions, the man's throne empty at my side,
my brow is glowing ruby-wreathed like the dawn-clouds,
my purple-tinted fingers, my drowsy almond eyes
shine like a god's as they strike down and raise;
what you found sweet and bitter I come to, I taste.

Orange veils on my shoulders, fireflower wreaths on my dark hair,
the reedpipe cries, the eunuchs drone, the altar's set.
Come Bulak-Amba my starry bull-browed ancestor!
Come Aure-Ange my lovely holy milk-rich ancestress!

Mango, areca, piled on the altar,
the year's brimming rice, brown coconut, white copra,
all round, red flower thrown on red flower,
sweet sandalwood fumes float up into the air.

Great man-spirit with no name: eat!
Great woman-spirit with no name: eat!
Huge emptiness in the silence behind the drumbeat: eat!

I call you, my father over the foam,
my old begetter, Batan-Kenam,
you are coming in your sun-chariot, four-elephant-drawn,
through the head-waving rattlesnakes of five cosmic storms,
my soldier, ageless, coral-garlanded,
blue-shirted arms,
lance of sky's shark-bone, turtle shield,
cut-off locks of the seven dancer-stars shimmer at your belt,
your elephants lumber and stamp, tiger-herds are felled,
and you rest on your elbow at the world's end in the lee of the
          loud blue mountain –
I salute you my glittering visitor, my far-off father!

I am wrapped in my veil, I am hidden,
the welcoming hostess is timid,
I hand out half-peeled oranges on a gold dish:
look at me here, I am your own flesh,
you know I am supple and clawed like a forest cat,
you pause if you see my dark green shining eyes,
my white-hot teeth-embers,
behind, my skeleton is lace-fine, a dragonfly:
see your one-day-old woman! one smile is all she would wish!

I summon you Aruvatene, my mother!
I call you. I am your daughter. Do you love her?
Your little one, will you be her protector?
Look, Nightqueen, at your tiny drop of dew:
the sparkling skin, the swelling breast!
You thick-starred heavenly palm tree, I dance for you.
Blow the pipe, roll the drum,
my dance-wind skims about you, let it come!
my silver ankle-jangle chatters – from you it came!
my orange shawl flies out – you gave it my name!

But if your beautiful face goes ashy as mist
I give you my blood to drink from your ancient chalice,
turn back, I leave you in peace,
eat, drink in silence.

Come too, Andede, good grandmother,
you are as old as the wind
that snuffles in the oven-cinders.
I shall never be so old,
fugitive with blowing flowers.

Andede, good grandmother,
you are as wrinkled as the stone
that snaps off from the mountain.
I shall never be so wrinkled,
I am the rock-escaping fountain.

Andede, good grandmother,
you smile like a yellow desert place
grinding its bones, toothless sand-cascades
skirting the cosmic border.
That is not my smile,
I am the lady of two empires,
sword and bread on my lap together
under the trickle of my tears.

Andede, good grandmother,
you champ and smack like the green dragon
that swallows up the wildest moor.
But I can never be satisfied,
two nations fight to eat from my hand
and bread forever lusts after sword.

Andede, good grandmother,
perpetually decaying, never destroyed,
you are puny but sinewy like a root in the earth,
I am the mother of everybody,
I would take them all on my lap,
I would let them all eat and sup,
but when I even raise my hand, I die.

Great man-spirit with no name: eat!
Great woman-spirit with no name: eat!
Huge emptiness in the silence behind the drumbeat: eat!

Come forward, now, great, ancient, unforgotten,
every sky-dome-breasted queen,
every lightning-dashing king!
I know that your good
is our only food,
but if misery surges again,
here I am – my blame alone,
I your shadow, your orphan,
prostrate under your cane,
beg for that bastinadoing!

For heaven's sake help me then!
Oh I am the virgin peahen
who instead of living eggs
found redhot stones between her legs
and with anxious wings spread wide
broods to hatch a void.
Pain of two nations is fire under me,
who will ever hatch the happiness of the world?

[EM]

Monkeyland

Oh for far-off monkeyland,
ripe monkeybread on baobabs,
and the wind strums out monkeytunes
from monkeywindow monkeybars.

Monkeyheroes rise and fight
in monkeyfield and monkeysquare,
and monkeysanatoriums
have monkeypatients crying there.

Monkeygirl monkeytaught
masters monkeyalphabet,
evil monkey pounds his thrawn
feet in monkeyprison yet.

Monkeymill is nearly made,
miles of monkeymayonnaise,
winningly unwinnable
winning monkeymind wins praise.

Monkeyking on monkeypole
harangues the crowd in monkeytongue,
monkeyheaven comes to some,
monkeyhell for those undone.

Macaque, gorilla, chimpanzee,
baboon, orangutan, each beast
reads his monkeynewssheet at
the end of each twilight repast.

With monkeysupper memories
the monkeyouthouse rumbles, hums,
monkeyswaddies start to march,
right turn, left turn, shoulder arms –

monkeymilitary fright
reflected in each monkeyface,
with monkeygun in monkeyfist
the monkeys' world the world we face.

[EM]

Ars Poetica

Memory cannot make your song everlasting.
Glory is not to be hoped from the evanescences:
how could it glorify you, when its glitterings are not essences?
Your song may flaunt a few embers from eternal things
while those who face them take fire as a minute passes.

Sages suggest: only individuals are in their senses.
All right; but to get more, be more than individual:
slip off your great-poet status, your lumbering galoshes,
serve genius, give it your human decencies
which are point and infinity: neither big nor small.

Catch the hot words that shine in the soul's estuaries:
they feed and sustain countless earth-centuries
and only migrate into your transient song,
their destiny is eternity as your destiny is,
they are friends who hug you and hasten soaring on.

[EM]

from The Lost Parasol

> *I think there is much more in even the smallest creation*
> *of God, should it only be an ant, than wise men think.*
> ST TERESA OF AVILA

Where metalled road invades light thinning air,
some twenty steps more and a steep gorge yawns
with its jagged crest, and the sky is rounder there,
    it is like the world's end;
nearer: bushy glade in flower,
farther: space, rough mountain folk;
    a young man called his lover
    to go up in the cool of daybreak,
they took their rest in the grass, they lay down;
the girl has left her red parasol behind.

Wood shades sunshade. Quietness all round.
What can be there, with no one to be seen?
Time pours out its measureless froth and
   the near and the far still unopened
   and midday comes and evening comes,
no midday there, no evening, eternal floods
that swim in the wind, the fog, the light, the world
and this tangle moves off into endlessness
like a gigantic shimmering silk cocoon,
skirted by wells of flame and craters of soot.

Dawn, a pearl-grey ferry, was drifting
   on its bright herd of clouds,
from the valley the first cow-bell came ringing
and the couple walked forward, head by head;
   now their souvenir clings to the shadows,
red silk, the leaves, the green light on it, filtering,
   metal frame, bone handle, button:
   separate thing from the order of men,
   it came home intact, the parasol,
its neighbours rockface and breeze, its land cold soil.

In a sun-rocked cradle which is as massive
as the very first creation itself
   the little one lies, light instrument
on the blue-grey mossy timber of a cliff,
around it the stray whistling, the eternal murmuring
of the forest, vast Turkey-oak, slim hornbeam,
briar-thickets, a thousand sloe-bushes quivering,
noble tranquil ranks of created things,
   and among them only the parasol flares out:
jaunty far-off visitor whose clothes still shout.

Languidly, as if long established there,
   its new home clasps it about:
the rocks hug their squat stonecrops,
above it the curly heliotropes
   cat's-tail veronica,
wild pinks push through cage of thistles,
dragon-fly broods on secret convolvulus,
   dries his gauze wings, totters out:
   so life goes on here, never otherwise −
a chink in the leaves, a flash of blue-smiling skies.

The huge-lunged forest breathes at it
   like yesterday, like long ago,
mild smell of the soft nest of a girl.
   Shy green woodpecker and russet
frisky squirrel refused to sit on it,
who knows what it hides: man left it;
but a nosy hedgehog comes up to the ledge,
the prickly loafer, low of leg,
like a steam puffer patrols round the rock;
puts heart in the woodpecker tapping at his trunk.

The sun stretches out its muscular rays:
you would expect the bell of heaven to crack.
Broad world – so many small worlds find their place
in you! Through the closed parasol's hills and valleys
an oblong speck moves: an ant that drags
the headless abdomen of a locust with rapt
persistence and effort: up to the bare heights,
down to the folds, holding the load tight,
and turning back at the very end of the way,
floundering up again with the body. Who knows why?

This finger-long journey is not shorter or sillier
than Everything, and its aim is just as hidden.
Look: through the branches you can see the hillside,
there a falcon, a spot on the clear sky,
hangs in the air like a bird of stone:
predator, hanging over from history.
Here, wolf and brown bear were once at home,
crystalline lynx lay in ambush for the innocent.
God wetted a finger, turned a page
and the world had a very different image.

A sky-splitting single-sloped precipice,
its lap a lemon-yellow corrie of sand,
far off a rosy panorama of mist,
curly hills in a ragged mauve cloud-band;
above, the couple stood; below, the sun-wheel stirred;
in the dawn-flames, so interdependent
they stood, afraid, at the very edge of fate;
boulders rolled from beneath their feet,
   they were quarrelling, tearing their hearts,
each of them deaf before the other starts.

In the tangled thicket of their young blood
the luminous world skulks off, sinks;
    shame like a rose-branch cut
       the boy to the quick:
beyond entreaty, ready to throw himself down to...
His white shirt gestured against the blue,
    at the shrubby scarp with its bindweed
       he lurched forward, forward
growing smaller and more distant – and his frightened girl
runs after him through briars, her knee's blood is a pearl.

Tall sedges lean over the gorge
and like a gemmed porch of the depths below
an army of tiny shining shields of weeds
    and a thick dark couch of green
cling round the bark of a stump that points no-
where, here their frenzy lost its rage:
they twined together, to ask why, to cry,
like the horned moon the white flash of a thigh;
    a hooded boletus at their feet
fattened its spore-crammed belly, not bothering to mate.

    The hilltop sends down
      wind tasting of stone
   to crochet sudden air-lace;
   and the lost parasol
    shivers and half lives;
in the endlessly intricate forest, in the deep maze
    of its undergrowth, a breeze
lurks, but takes off at the sharp rock-fall,
pouring over that solitary wall
and across the ravine, flying light to the dale.

    Zigzag mane of the thicket
      wavers and swirls,
    the forest depths are sighing,
a thousand tiny leaves, like birds' tails, flicker
    and glint in the light like scales;
drawn up from a breeze-wakened copse
yeasty, spicy fragrances are flying;
    a snapped thorn-branch stirs, drops,
      catches on the soft fabric:
on the tent-like parasol the first tear is pricked.

No one is sorry –
right above it an oriole is calling,
   inside it a bow-legged spider scurries
   round and round the scarlet corrie
and makes off: under the metal-arched ribs
a lizard twists in search of his siesta,
   he guzzles the oven-heat and like a jester
   propped on both hands peeps out from the midst;
   later some mice come running in and out
and the shaft has a gaudy tit perking about.

In the vault of summer skies, diamond-blue,
an ice-white lace-mist moves in a smile;
over the plain, at the foothills of heaven,
there are dark woolpacks hanging heavy
and truant cloud-lines in crumbling style;
Apollo, body stripped, striding through,
   runs young, strong, and fresh,
hot oil steams on the earth's rough flesh;
in air that rocks both valley and peak,
in empty immensities – a red spot of silk.

The girl of the neglected parasol
   is just as small, lost in the broad world,
a tiny insect dropped in a sea-wide flood;
   no one to talk to at all,
wrapping her own soul round her fear,
   she curls up in a curtained room,
and hears a whipped dog whining there
as if there was no misery anywhere,
no other wound to ache in earth or heaven;
or does he howl for all the pain of men?

       Hanging on the sky's arch
        at the lower bank
          the dusk
          is hazy.
   The first? How many before? On the lazy
ridge no grass or insect measures it,
neither cuckoo nor cuckoo-spit,
the twilights turn for ever, as created.
  At the rock's edge, with forever's speed
the sleek silk vanishes into foaming shade.

Night's victory, yesterday's goodbye:
huge galley in the bay of earth and sky,
floating catafalque of dead Osiris;
scarlet embers fall into saffron high-tide,
peacock of air bends his fan from the heights,
shimmering feathers are roses and night-stocks;
an organ of gold installed in space
opens up all its pipes and lips,
pencils of light-rays spring from the rifts
and stroke the hills while darkness fills their cliffs.

On the foamy crest of foliage
light and shade come knotted together
like the body's pain and pleasure.
Fading now, from its cover, the cuckoo's message,
and the motley unison
of piping, chattering, chirping, splashing
prankishness and passion.
The evening light, that turns dreams on,
bends through the cool slow-surging trees,
gleams in the silvery homespun of twittering beaks.

[EM]

Mural of the 20th Century

Castles in the air,
filled for three thousand years with decorations and junk,
with chests bearing inscriptions – 'mine', 'I', 'for me', 'me',
their walls bulging with 'my treasure', 'my fever', 'my salvation'
it all finally toppled
and fell into the dung piled up below.

Its inhabitants
throng in the dirt down there,
not understanding what happened, not seeing in the night,
struggling on the garbage with heavy moans or

scurrying tread on each other
carrying their broken, creaking belongings
they want to build by devastating the ruins –

But there is one among them who can see
and rolling himself in tar he sets himself on fire
that they too should see:
desperate light, live torch.

Some point at him: 'Look at the fool,
he dipped himself in tar and now burns to ashes
instead of helping us salvage.'
Others yell: 'We can see by his light'
and they drag and pull the broken junk still faster.

What could they see? What could the live torch show them?
the ruins, the dung
and above it the black nothing
where the castle in the air has already vanished
and the angels also have vanished,
the Angels of Security, of Freedom, of Truth, and of everything
          else
even the Angel of War is gone, for what they take down there for
          war
is a ceaseless squabbling in the dark
of people tumbling against one another;
where is the time when free decision declared the war?
and even the Angel of Hatred is gone –
everybody bites any leg he can –
where is true hatred now?

One remains in the sky, an idle, indifferent soul
the Angel of Disgust, for now only disgust
still has a soul.

If they could see by the light of the live torch
they would see him, the Angel of Disgust,
as he dangles his legs for dogs or whistling
urinates on the ruins,
and would not believe he is an angel
that he is love in a new shape, who smiles and does not anger
and if they saw him close up they would not believe

he is the Angel of Disgust, for he is as beautiful
as the woman carried in the depths of our dreams,
the murderer falls into ecstasy, throws himself on his fists
and makes solemn promises, and the pure man too is startled:
and the shouting torch of fire and the final sweetness
are one and the same –

If they ask him, he answers:
'Don't meddle' pouting his lips he says 'Don't meddle.'
And he says it a third time, 'Don't meddle.' And grows silent.

The live torch runs around and shouts –
'Have you heard – don't meddle!
These two words are the word flown to you, they are the Great
        Book,
these two words could smooth the convulsions of the world.
Don't meddle, don't long to sway banners,
nor to fling up your arms with the motions
of building, of destroying, of salvaging,
leave slogans alone, self-important principles, convulsive ideas.
Listen – demand no advantage,
don't believe for the sake of advantage
and the hundred madnesses which promise advantage
will fall away from you,
and you will be like the heart-beat:
its calm is activity and its activity a calm.'

Having shouted this, the live torch collapsed,
ashes and soot pour from his mouth,
even his bones are black.

The Angel of Disgust
dispassionately plays
above the ruins.
He is waiting.

[RL]

LÁSZLÓ KÁLNOKY

What Man Can Do on This Planet

To kindle fire so that the flame,
when flaring, should bite our hands.

To suffer thirst so that after the first gulp
the glass should absorb water.

To run along a corridor
streaked by shrill lunatic cries
without losing our sanity.

To fall down ensnared by lights
waiting for the weapon to strike
or for a reprieve granted by the mercy
of him who misunderstood our countenance.

To nettle indifference with provocative words
just when it was turning away from us.

Vegetating in the colourless matter
of danger that you get accustomed to,
to find a secret window
and to divine the blurred picture
of the town five hundred years from now.

Even with plugged ears
to listen to muffled, unknown voices
and answer them
even with your mouth gagged.

[GG]

The Fatties at the Baths

The sun prowls impatient of its own heat
and kindles the coal deep under ground.
We pant for coolness. But the baths have a weight
of stricken monoliths, stranded slugs, all round

the water's edge, where the heavy fat ones lie;
they sprawl on their backs, growing slowly ripe
like huge fruits in their steam conservatory,
while stubble makes black chins you cannot wipe.

Their chest-hair's thickly matted like dark scrub
a jungle for the wandering ants to explore;
their belly and their forehead have the daub
of red the summer sun makes roses for.

Sweat seeps into the furrows of their fat
and trickles down like greasy, ropy tears,
but gathers in their navel's little vat;
purple apoplexy bulges behind their ears.

The mirage somersaults and shimmers away.
Their heads take a hundred thousand white
steel-rays, reeds like metal in a glittering spray.
The water boils, bursts into flame. Noontide!

Nine angels blow their blistering trumpet-brass,
but the bathers have gone deaf to such appeals,
their vacant watery eyes watch nothing pass,
their consciousness sinks in unfathomed wells.

They lie there peacefully, waiting perhaps
for the sun to suck up their obesity,
and on a light ray, a thread that never snaps,
like indolent balloons, they'd fly away.

[EM]

The Translator's Death

Twenty years further on, what will I be like?
I think of it more and more, with less and less delight.
Hacked and battered, grey and bald, thin as a rake,
my study an espresso-bar for old times' sake,
I'll sit there scribbling, to cup after cup
of caffeine euphoria, my artery walls
growing sclerotic and silting up
just to remind me of coffins and palls.
Yet it's not the embolism, the cerebral haemorrhage
that brings the threat. My end is more strange:
the lifelong translator must leave the stage
shot like the mark on a rifle-range.

When I die, I hope you will all laugh out loud,
don't let pity lie on your hearts like a cloud.
Pass your strictest judgements upon me:
'Well, at last this fool has got his fee,
he knew what he was after, pouring his life's blood
into a succession of alien spirits, proud
to meet a new commission for his pen
by slicing his heart like an onion-skin.
What if it was his sweet treasure, his talent, he chose
to sell it mercilessly, like glucose.
And so he emptied himself bit by bit
till he was a bag of bones...which broke and split.
And now? He's ripe and ready for trash city.'
Don't hold me back with mercy, don't give me pity!

[EM]

Findings

1

spun round by the bandstand strains
the hanged man
swings like a pendulum –
where the brass trumpets
lie among the shrubs
the moonlight on its evening stroll
pauses and muses

2

the armchair dust puffs up
and covers thought with its grey powder
the toes of an immovably silent
wooden leg are being thumbscrewed
at this moment by a patient inquisition

3

what are those insects sipping
from my half-emptied glass
while the shadow plaits its absurd
chastity-belt on the fruitless
sculpted loins of Polyhymnia

4

it seems I shall never take
the steps that would lead me
into my heart of hearts
to find out
if the chronic gangrene
gnawing away there
is an epidemic or my own affair

[EM]

ZOLTÁN JÉKELY

To My Bones

I live my life from day to day as if
about to sleep for ever, dreamily
watching bones that have jogged along with me
and which my soul's so rudely set to leave.

My skull which has been of little or no use
this hundred years under its weight of clay
now cracks in three, a spring shower sweeps away
dusty heaps of poems like so much refuse.

My teeth corroded over twenty years
by rich food, eaten through by acids, glow
uncannily in row by rotten row
under the earth, sad timeless souvenirs.

My spine, with its length of crackling vertebrae
through which blood pounded, now the marrow's gone
is hollow, perhaps a snake might try it on
or roots provide a line to dangle by.

My poor hand, which I used to love to sniff
after it had explored another's skin,
no use you beckoning to the man within,
poor hand, for you, like him, are trapped and stiff.

And you, my legs, young puppies, you who'd squeeze
a female leg, or kick a football high,
for ever at attention now you'll lie
nor graveyard sergeant give you the At ease.

[GSz]

Towards the New Millennium

It's not the year two-thousand, my poor love,
the new millenium has not come upon us;
we're asleep in the deep though the old blue above
is buzzing with a strange new apparatus.
The house where we were born has been knocked flat,
whole districts downed. Our beds and chairs are dust.
Our books are gone (foul hands have seen to that)
our likenesses in art are likewise lost.
New shoes are squeaking down the avenue:
the girls are different, their clothes different too.
Our dreams, like old wine too long bottled, thicken
and grow sweet, till their very flavours sicken.
Time dangles the sun on its slow pendulum
above the earth. And when at last we come
to sleep, it's as if in some distant zone
like long-boned Incas swaddled in the stone.

[GSz]

Dragon Slaying

That hideous overgrown toad again!
How it croaks through the night, in the silence!
It blares in my ear, it fills my apartment –
already I see its dull yellow eyes before me.
But where is it hidden, what nook, or what sewer?
Where's its rolling belly, that monstrosity,
show me so I can kick it or grind it under!

How soundly the town sleeps,
the panting spirits of tired humanity
tumble softly across the wide pavement,
their dreams are fumbling at clouded
windowpanes – are joined in one outsize
dream of peace rising slowly to heaven.
And look, we must hear that terror again
right from the beginning, in the silence!
Is it in rutting mood, seeking a loathsome partner
to reproduce its repulsive image? –

From a gateway it belches into view, its huffing
belly in full croak – I see it! Disgust and fury
pursue me as I run, and I
grab at a half-brick, and smash it as hard
as I can, into his horrible body – death to all such! –
and I can still see its guts spilling out,
how they ripple in coils in the half-light,
and its monstrous eye keeps staring at me,
I, who was born on the day of St George who
once slew the dragon, and has again slain it.

[GSz]

GYŐZŐ HATÁR

The Shot Hare

Hare Like
He flies before the volley, riddled through
As I, my Lord, being wounded, flee from You

On Film
A vast crowd gathers to observe the game
As you release the safety catch, take aim

Screen
The gamekeepers are cherubim; they ring
Us round in choirs, wildly signalling

The Kill
Your angels too forget their customed hymns:
From lofty tribunes rise their mingled screams

Three
I leapt three Himalayas, but I found
None of Your vaunted mercy, no safe ground

I Fear
My ears pinned back, I strain hare-ears to hear
(The hare's own shadow knows enough of fear)

Report
The firing stills my terror. 'Brave wee chap!
His glossy coat would make a winter cap
To crown the Milky Way.' The hammers tap,

They nail me up, but I'm not quite done in:
My skin may yet suffice to save my skin.

[GSz]

Fidelity

the word this word's mere ghosting bass
my life I'll haunt you every place

    fidelity life-sanctifying fidelity
    heart shaking beauty-ecstasy

though others sell it, or sleep it through:
I'll bear it nor forswear it – here's work to do

    fidelity life-sanctifying fidelity
    heart rending beauty-ecstasy

that myself and my body be wholly immersed in it
let work only work be the last and the first in it

    fidelity life-sanctifying fidelity
    heart rending beauty-ecstasy

In intellect and soul engraved, deep seated:
I desire that labour never be completed

Unfooted, snow-white, spotless
my wings, bond-brotherliness

    fidelity life-sanctifying fidelity
    heart rending beauty-ecstasy

[GSz]

Identifications

monkey monkey monkey monkey
      locked away in monkey shape
myself am locked up under one key
      inside a solitary ape
consciousness self knowledge cannot
      worm however hard it tries
out of its monkey skin and phizzog,
      monkey fur, face, ear and eyes.

spider will remain a spider,
      catfish gawp as catfish do,
you'll not cut yourself from inside or
      shed your skin by slicing through!
ants are ants and have to stick it
      gladly though they'd flee the heap
walk two legged through the wicket,
      or sprout avian wings and cheep –

on your neighbour's skull go knocking:
      its chitin armour will not give!
friend! my body needs defrocking!
      one must change if one's to live!
How keen we are to swap our tallies
      with any likeness! Oh our dust
might yet be human, though our bellies
      heave with the old toad of lust

life gulps, grasps, slobbers, croaks and jostles:
      all gut! a thousand mortal tussles!
and from disgust's amphibian roe
      the glooms of pantheism grow.

[GSz]

The Flame Gone Out

I loved you, world, I loved you desperately
I loved you, I doted on being alive
you guided me to gather and make thrive
unquenchable, first real reality

you commanded me to love the terrible
dangers of existence, light of your sun
and night of your moon, my wholesale consumption,
for you I was insatiable

this was how the bondage of becoming
became for us a cursed affair
your task for me was prayer:
fidelity and beauty blossoming

I had to beseech you: let me still continue!
I dote on living: distribute life and weigh it!
I'd round up your numbers, make them complete
do not scorn my wolfish greed for you

not in my loves, not in music, nor
in the thundering of heavy artillery:
in your scheme of Last Things let me
try to melt back, separate no more.

I clutched and held as much as I could grasp:
this pittance in the palm of my brain
through the glass of indifference, my glass faith may gain
a new reality in death, one I can clasp

My eyes grow wide consuming you, prostrate
I will not seek you, nor swear by my success,
in ambiguities, delusions, deviousness
be merciless, transparent distillate

with one crack of your whip, you whipped me into line
eyes, ears, all five senses I gained by your grace
so you became the vast expanse of space
an endless prodigal bank of fact and sign

I merely catalogue you, reckon up your all
bewitched, inscrutable phenomenon,
whelping forth, productive daily cauldron!
pediment topped by sun or star-dial!

no lees from the wine-press could compense us for your loss
no wretched deathly *post hoc* of the soul,
but you within me, and I within the whole:
let being enter being in one round cosmos!

however slyly approaches the hour
with its monsters and cancers whatever the choice
only for you will I raise my voice
cry, hold on! to perception and to power!

unquenchable, first real reality
you guided me to gather and make thrive
I loved you, I doted on being alive
I loved you, world, I loved you desperately

[GSz]

London Lament
'for a tyrant'

She runs her gamut of enticements, wields her treacly charms
my *deariedums*, my *sweetikins*, my *love-come-to-my-arms*

so lavishly she pets and preens, so lavishly she flatters
she gives her all, asks no returns, it's yours, it hardly matters

her strictly legal honeycombs, her paradise of treats
who'd argue with a tyrant so replete with scents and sweets

demands are couched in gentle terms, obsequious request,
her discipline is just as mild: your study, room arrest

prodigal with her radiance, her panaceas of cheer
the lady with the linament! one glance – pains disappear

like horses they stand, neck on neck, frozen in a kiss
and would remain so evermore. epitomes of bliss

they'd stay like this for ever, *requiescat in pace*,
their feet resting on little dogs, one stone dog for each party

two guardian angels to prepare their beds in the stone choir
inscribe: Behold! Here lie the Lord and Lady of the shire

*

but when the fit is on her then her fiery eyes grow mean
the steely glance becomes a blade, Madame la Guillotine

her mood flares florid, frosty broadsides brook no interruption
her ready fret and fury shows the tyrant in eruption

It isn't done? Where have you put it? Am I supposed to find it?
(She makes it clear what is your stuff and where she has consigned it.)

spend all this money? pay so much? when this won't feed a fly?
such trivial botching? this? you call this housework, darling? why?

so this is how a man does housework? what is so amusing?
the dusty sideboard, the creased pillow both look on accusing

a filthy mess, a leaking pipe, a fire in the attic?
a fine homecoming! you are so annoying, so pathetic

and when she flings her locks back and shakes them in a fit
be sure she'll smack her *babyboo*, she'll lord-and-lady it

a dripping rope, a cycle chain – mechanics of command
sirrah, the whip! the fool is beat, the lash lies close to hand

though other times it's *sweetiepie*, or *sweetiedums* or *sweetie*,
should gravy slop on his new suit the treatment's beyond entreaty

a soft boiled egg might smear his cuff eliciting a slap
black forest gateau sadly slip and slither in his lap

She only has to turn the key, her footsteps are a caution
– when they are heavy – he can forecast what will be his portion

sweetiepoops's shirt's askew, his bellybutton peeping,
let him scuff and potter about all night without sleeping

moustache is a bedraggled tail, his duck's arse mane is spiky,
infuriating his whole being, his coxcombly psyche

sweetiepoops but opens his mouth in unpropitious dither
a hefty swipe makes one earring, the wall slams on the other

should he grimace or should he grin, he shifts from foot to foot
his essence shrinks and fits her palm, he's shrivelled and minute

heel already bound behind him, waist snapped, suicidal
the strap off his own back provides a useful bit and bridle

a thumbscrew wanted? it's on tap no need to go and fetch
behold the female tyrant, public hangdame, Ms Jack Ketch

*

but when the turning of the lock portends a gentler mood
you'll kiss the gilt edge of her cape with mild solicitude

she goes on tiptoe, little scamp, her little hooves clipclopping,
comes dripping with a Christmas tree and gifts of copious shopping

here are twopence-coloured books, postcards in profusion
(the tyranny is inhumane yet blessed with constitution)

no need to eat and drink she'll blithely waive necessity
in her be-gâteauxed, clownish, imperial capacity

like horses they stand, neck on neck, frozen in a kiss
and would remain so evermore: epitomes of bliss

they'd stay like this for ever, *requiescat in pace*,
their feet resting on little dogs, one stone dog for each party

smiling, all-embracing, serene, all things at her beck
the swelling cello of her hips the viol of her neck

it is a yoke, it weighs one down and yet how it bewitches
a sleight of hand decapitates, the headless body twitches

her burden's joy, her tyranny diversion in a wife,
you'll snug down with her in her nest within the Tree of Life

[GSz]

Vampire

once in the course of my stealthy expeditions, my
capacious cloaked circumambulations, I happened on a heart-
rendingly beautiful Neck of Improbable Length

my eyes glued to it I lapped up this vision of the Neck
and like a drunk mathematician calculated the three possible
uses to which I could put it

the first. I would kiss it until it choked and she expired
in my Kisses Appropriate to Long Necks

the second. As we adhered to one another in the course of
the kiss I would sink my teeth in and bite through Longstem

the third. Instead of kissing her to death or biting her in
two I would hold her at arm's length, strangle her and visually
enjoy the long death agonies of Longstem

in the end I chose the fourth course. I married her

ever since then, day and night, I have lived under the
spell of this Neck of Improbable Length. I can never exhaust my
appetite for its contours

often it happens that I cling to her in such a mad ecstasy
of love that I forget to listen to what she is saying and I
don't understand her. Then she gets very angry:

You're not listening to what I am saying. What did I say?
You pay no attention to me...

Silently I hear out the buzz of her accusations but my
ears are tuned to her neck now rather then her throat, and –

say it now! say it now! once more! – I cry. And she repeats
her accusations gurgling and cackling under my kisses

(by the way) partly, (since it is through my sensuous
parts I have proceeded part by part along her and tasted all
the flavours of her neck), partly through my kiss-sensors I have
sought out her jugular. Now! Now! the thought has flashed
through my fangs, now I ought to cut short her life, to put an
end to her struggles. Now! Now!...but she dropped her fourfold
blonde portcullis over my eyes and I found myself in a golden
cage. As Odysseus clung to the ram that saved his life, so she
battened her arms and legs around me in a brainstorm of embraces;
though I was practically there, her carotid pulsing between
my canines – too late. I had the perfect opportunity and missed it.
Instead, scorpion fashion, I injected my stinging tail into
her from below, and once I was sure that I could penetrate no
deeper I released my paralysing poison. I ordered the flooding
of her cavities and marshalled an ejaculation

she gave herself up to death by ecstasy and obediently
accommodated her pelvic rhythm to our mutual dying. When we
woke from our corpses there were three of us; but only in an
emblematic sense, heralding only a pair of twins, otherwise
there might have been a whole army of them like a set of organ
pipes. And beside me on the pillow there still stretched the
long slender junoesque Neck

– You obstinate, you roughneck! – I continued gently,
twisting the rough word into her neckverse, just as I had
always sharpened my knowledge of vernacular rhetoric on her.
You Neck! You've got a 'neck': even without your ornaments you
have an Ornamental Neck!

– And you, you're all tongue: leave me alone! You cling to
me like a necklace...!

I don't remember her face, I never saw it. I carried the
majestic vision of
the Neck with me into my cinerarium which is
cast in the form of Isis the Earth Mother, and I mingled my
dust with hers in the jar – eternal peace measured to its
precise length.

[GSz]

JÁNOS PILINSZKY

Complaint

Buried alive under the stars
in the mud of nights
do you hear my dumbness?
as if a skyful of birds were approaching.

I keep up this wordless appeal.
Will you ever unearth me
from the perpetual silence
under your foreign skies?

Does my complaint reach you?
Is my siege futile?
All around me glitter
reefs of fear.

Only let me count on you, God.
I want your nearness so much,
shivering
makes the love of loves even fierier.

Bury me in your embrace.
Do not leave me to the frost.
Even if my air is used up
my calling will not tire.

Be the bliss of my trembling
like a tree's leaves:
give a name, give a beautiful name
a pillow to this disintegration.

[TH/JC]

By the Time You Come

I am alone. And by the time you come
I shall be the only one still alive.
Feathers in an empty roost.
Stars intead of a sky.

In my orphanage, unburied
as on a wintry dump
picking among the rubbish
I keep finding scraps of my life.

And that will be seamless peace.
Even my heart inaudible.
All around me the ecstatic
barriers of silence.

Naked eternity.
And yours, helplessly yours.
A majestic simplicity
created for you, from the first day.

Like a lumpish basketwork dummy
time simply sits, without a word.
Desire has lost its limbs.
It has nothing but a gasping trunk.

By the time you come I shall have lost everything.
No house, no soft bed.
We shall be able to lie undisturbed
in a bare ecstasy.

Only you must not rob me, you must not desert me.
If you are weak, I am finished.
Horrible, then, to awake, in a bed
among pillows, hearing the noise of the street.

[TH/JC]

Harbach 1944

(to Gábor Thurzó)

At all times I see them.
The moon brilliant. A black shaft looms up.
Beneath it, harnessed men
haul a huge cart.

Dragging that giant wagon
which grows bigger as the night grows
their bodies are divided among
the dust, their hunger and their trembling.

They are carrying the road, they are carrying the land,
the bleak potato fields,
and all they know is the weight of everything,
the burden of the skylines

and the falling bodies of their companions
which almost grew into their own
as they lurch, living layers,
treading each other's footsteps.

The villages stay clear of them,
the gateways withdraw.
The distance, that has come to meet them,
reels away back.

Staggering, they wade knee deep
in the low, darkly-muffled clatter
of their wooden clogs
as through invisible leaf litter.

Already their bodies belong to silence.
And they thrust their faces towards the height
as if they strained for a scent
of the far-off celestial troughs

because, prepared for their coming
like an opened stock-yard,
its gates flung savagely back,
death gapes to its hinges.

[TH/JC]

On the Wall of a KZ-Lager

Where you have fallen, you stay.
In the whole universe, this is your place.
Just this single spot.
But you have made this yours utterly.

The countryside evades you.
House, mill, poplar,
each thing strives to be free of you
as if it were mutating in nothingness.

But now it is you who stay.
Did we blind you? You continue to watch us.
Did we rob you? You enriched yourself.
Speechless, speechless, you testify against us.

[TH/JC]

November Elysium

Convalescence. You hang back, at the verge
of the garden. Your background
a peaceful yellow wall's monastery silence.
A tame little wind starts out across the grass. And now.
as if hands assuaged them with holy oils,
your five open wounds, your five senses
feel their healing and are eased.

You are timid. And exultant. Yes,
with your childishly translucent limbs,
in the shawl and coat grown tall,
you are like Alyosha Karamazov.

And like those gentle ones, over yonder,
who are like the child, yes, you are like them.
And as happy too, because
you do not want anything any more.
Only to gleam like the November sun,
and exhale fragrance, lightly as a fir-cone.
Only to bask, like the blest.

[TH/JC]

Fable
(from KZ-Oratorio: Dark Heaven)

Once upon a time
there was a lonely wolf
lonelier than the angels.

He happened to come to a village.
He fell in love with the first house he saw.

Already he loved its walls
the caresses of its bricklayers.
But the window stopped him.

In the room sat people.
Apart from God nobody ever
found them so beautiful
as this child-like beast.

So at night he went into the house.
He stopped in the middle of the room
and never moved from there any more.

He stood all through the night, with wide eyes
and so into the morning when he was beaten to death.

[TH/JC]

Epilogue
(to Pierre Emmanuel)

Remember? On the faces.
Remember? The empty ditch.
Remember? It's streaming down.
Remember? I stand in the sun.

You read the Paris Journal.
Since then, winter has come. Winter's night.
You lay the table beside me.
You make the bed in the moonlight.

Catching your breath, you undress
in the dark of the bare house.
You let down your skirt, and take off your blouse.
Your back is a bare tombstone.

Image of wretched strength.
Is anybody here?
                    A waking dream:
unanswered, I cross
the rooms lying in the depths of mirrors.

Is this my face? This face?
The light, the silence, and the judgement are shattered
as this stone, my face, hurtles towards me
out of the snow-white mirror!

And the horsemen! The horsemen!
Darkness oppresses me. The lamplight hurts me.
A slack thread of water plays
on the motionless china.

I rattle at the closed doors.
Your room is dark as a shaft.
The walls glare with cold.
I smudge my weeping on the wall.

You snow-heaped house-tops, help me!
Now it is night. Now let every orphaned thing
shine out, before there arises
the sun of nothingness. And you, in vain,

shine! I lean my head to the wall.
From all around me the dead city
holds towards me, mercy towards the dead,
a handful of snow.

I loved you! A shout. A sigh.
A cloud in flight.
And through the slush, under breaking dawn,
at a heavy torrential trot, come the horsemen.

[TH/JC]

Apocrypha

1

Everything will be forsaken then

The silence of the heavens will be set apart
and forever apart
the broken-down fields of the finished world,
and apart
the silence of dog-kennels.
In the air a fleeing host of birds.
And we shall see the rising sun
dumb as a demented eye-pupil
and calm as a watching beast.

But keeping vigil in banishment
because that night
I cannot sleep I toss
as the tree with its thousand leaves
and at dead of night I speak as the tree:

Do you know the drifting of the years
the years over the crumpled fields?
Do you understand the wrinkle
of transience? Do you comprehend
my care-gnarled hands? Do you know
the name of the orphanage? Do you know

what pain treads the unlifting darkness
with cleft hooves, with webbed feet?
The night, the cold, the pit. Do you know
the convict's head twisted askew?
Do you know the caked troughs, the tortures
of the abyss?

The sun rose. Sticks of trees blackening
in the infra-red of the wrathful sky.
So I depart. Facing devastation
a man is walking, without a word.
He has nothing. He has his shadow.
And his stick. And his prison garb.

2

And this is why I learned to walk! For these
belated bitter steps.

Evening will come, and night will petrify
above me with its mud. Beneath closed eyelids
I do not cease to guard this procession
these fevered shrubs, their tiny twigs.
Leaf by leaf, the glowing little wood.
Once Paradise stood here.
In half-sleep, the renewal of pain:
to hear its gigantic trees.

Home – I wanted finally to get home –
to arrive as he in the Bible arrived.
My ghastly shadow in the courtyard.
Crushed silence, aged parents in the house.
And already they are coming, they are calling me,
my poor ones, and already crying,
and embracing me, stumbling –
the ancient order opens to readmit me.
I lean out on the windy stars.

If only for this once I could speak with you
whom I loved so much. Year after year
yet I never tired of saying over
what a small child sobs
into the gap between the palings,

the almost choking hope
that I come back and find you.
Your nearness throbs in my throat.
I am agitated as a wild beast.

I do not speak your words,
the human speech. There are birds alive
who flee now heart-broken
under the sky, under the fiery sky.
Forlorn poles stuck in a glowing field,
and immovably burning cages.
I do not speak your language.
My voice is more homeless than the word!
I have no words.

          Its horrible burden
tumbles down through the air –
a tower's body emits sounds.

You are nowhere. How empty the world is.
A garden chair, and a deckchair left outside.
Among sharp stones my clangorous shadow.
I am tired. I jut out from the earth.

   3

God sees that I stand in the sun.
He sees my shadow on stone and on fence.
He sees my shadow standing
without a breath in the airless press.

By then I am already like the stone;
a dead fold, a drawing of a thousand grooves,
a good handful of rubble
is by then the creature's face.

And instead of tears, the wrinkles on the faces
trickling, the empty ditch trickles down.

[TH/JC]

Quatrain

Nails asleep under frozen sand.
Nights soaked in poster-loneliness.
You left the light on in the corridor.
Today my blood is shed.

[TH/JC]

Enough

Creation, no matter how vast,
is more cramped than a roost.
From here to there. Stone, tree, house.
I potter about, come early, come too late.

Yet, now and again, some person enters
and in a moment everything has opened –
the sight of a face, a presence is enough,
and the wallpaper starts to bleed.

Enough, yes, enough a hand
as it stirs a cup of coffee
or as it 'withdraws from the introduction'
and enough
that we forget the place
the airless row of windows, yes,
that returning, at night, to our room
we accept the unacceptable.

[TH/JC]

ÁGNES NEMES NAGY

Trees

It's time to learn. The winter trees.
How head to toe they're clad in frost.
Stiff monumental tapestries.

It's time to learn that region where
the crystal turns to steam and air,
and where the trees swim through the mist
like something remembered but long lost.

The trees, and then the stream behind,
the wild duck's silent sway of wing,
the deep blue night, white and blind,
where stand the hooded tribe of things,
here one must learn the unsung deeds
of heroism of the trees.

[GSz]

Statues

Statues I carried on board,
vast faces unnamed and unspanned,
statues I carried on board
to the island where they should stand.
Between nose and ear there were ninety
degrees, measured precisely,
with no other sign of their rank,
statues I carried on board,
and so I sank.

[GSz]

Bird

On my shoulder squats a bird
conjoined at birth, our souls allied,
grown so vast and burdensome
I'm racked with pain at every stride.

He weighs me down, he weighs and numbs.
I'd shoo him off, he'll not be shook.
He is an oak that sinks its roots
he digs his claws in me like hooks.

I hear his awful avian heart
drumming at my ear and know
I'd topple over like a log
if he were now to up and go.

[GSz]

Diary

Mind

I know I have no reasonable grounds
for thinking, but watch the thoughts as they go round.
And since contempt's appropriate to the act
mindlessly I trust to intellect.

Nightmare

From a world of rotting rags and clout
the marsh-light of cold reason flashes out,
plays on the corpse, the softening skull beneath,
and illuminates its naked row of teeth.

Revenge

He who cannot take revenge,
nor yet forgive, must find redress
in burning for ever the low flame
of his unquenchable bitterness.

Sic Itur ad Astra

Compared with these I am a saint,
   no judge would dare try me,
if the world wags on like this
   they will deify me.

July

Light and light and sunspots, fragrant colours,
in place of my heart *de rigeur* – bouquets.
Just this once, dear world, I will forgive you,
but from now on you'll have to mend your ways!

You Sit and Read

You sit and you read. How alone you are, even you don't know.
But sometimes you guess and then with a leisurely movement,
and a hint of mild animal sadness your simple features
dip into the light.

In Front of the Mirror

You take your face and slowly remove the paint,
but would remove the face that fate assigned you,
you wait for the armchair to rise and with a faint
gesture of boredom to appear behind you.

Contemplative

The old pose lost its charm. Let's take
a new one out. Yes, this will do.
In matters of dress it's all the same
what you fit your body to.
The dress, the body and the soul,
the same applies to everything.
When Thespis prinks, does she at all
suspect what change the colours bring?

Sincerity

Inspecting myself makes me bilious.
It's easier for the spontaneous.
I would if I could, be the driver of the dray
who washes great blonde horses all the day
and has nothing to say.

[GSz]

The Sleeping Horsemen
(to Lajos Kassák)

December. Noon. Eye-scorching
snowfield broad as a hillside.
On the flat slope a heap of flagstone.
On its round edges
a hot, white, snowsheet:
a small pile of sleeping Bedouins.

What faces are these that bend
groundward, dark shrubs,
in this inverted sculptural group?
What dried-up, black
root-features, what
hot, dark breathing –

And deep down under the shore
what kind of Bedouin horses,
their shapes here and there heaving,
as inside the stable corridors,
silently, invisibly, they paw,
and their root-bearded large manes
begin to sway underground –

And what is this motion when
on the hot earth-horses' backs
the earthy brown trunks stretch,
leafy-haired, higher and higher,
and with one slow stupendous leap
spring out.

[BB]

To My Craft

My craft, bewitching one,
you make me believe my life matters.
Between morality and terror, at the same time
in broad daylight and pitch blackness,

like a land with its cliffs mangled
by lightning, where the unstable weather
of immense clouds – huge cumulous
brains – clap their fire together,

and, in the fire-streaked air
they give birth to the endless battle,
the never-ending siege of Buda,
I've known since I was a cell,

where everything vibrates and is perishable,
where everything is basted, fraying, furred,
where the heart itself frazzles,
and on a single thread hangs the word,

the word that from earth to heaven
pendulums continuously its crackling, loud,
reverberating rhythm, conjoining
its own convulsions and the cloud –

between morality and terror,
or else in immoral terror,
my craft, for all that, it's you
that measures, that's beyond measure,

even if convulsively, but like a clock
that taps out illusory rhythms despite
its equable tick-tick – nonetheless
you divide the light from the night.

[BB]

To a Poet

My contemporary. He died, not I.
He fell near Tobruk, poor boy.
He was English. Other names, for us,
tell the places where, like ripe nuts,
heads fell and cracked in twos,
those portable radios,
their poise of parts and volume
finer than the Eiffel, lovely spinal column
as it crashed down to the earth.
That's how I think of your youth –
like a dotard who doesn't know
now from fifty years ago,
his heart in twilight, addlepated.

But love is complicated.

[BB]

Between

The great sleeves of air,
air on which the bird
and the science of birds bear
themselves, wings on the fraying argument;
incalculable result
of a moment's leafy silhouette
bark and branch of a haze living upwards
like desire into the upper leaves
to inhale every three seconds
those big, frosty angels.

Downweight. On the plain
the mountain's motionless shocks
as they lie or kneel
peaks and escarpments,
geology's figure-sculpture,
the glen's a moment's distraction
and once more the forms and rocks,
chalky bone to outline
into identity of pleated stone.

Between the sky and the earth.

Creaking of rocks. As
the sun's clear ores
into themselves almost, stone into metal, as
a creature steps on in his claws smoke,
and up above the escarpment
ribbons of burning hoof,
then night in the desert, night as
quenching and reaching
its stony core, night below zero, and as
the tendons, joints, plaques

split and tear, as
they are strained in endless
splitting ecstasy
by routine dumb lightning
in black and white −

Between the day and the night.

Aches and stabbings,
visions, voiceless aquaducts,
inarticulate risings,
unbearable tension
of verticals between up and down.

Climates. Conditions.
Between. Stone. Tanktraces.
A strip of black reed rimming the plain
written in two lines, in the lake, the sky,
two black plaques of signsystem,
diacritic on the stars –

Between the sky and the sky.

[HM]

Akhenaton in Heaven

All these things there are the same. The mine.
A mountainside torn to the foot. Implements.
As he touches the limestone
the dawn's uncertain.
As if dawning from inside,
on the rock's thin face,
and stone and iron transparent
as after an ultimate disfunction.

There the forest.
The fog walks about in fragments.
Five-fingered, like abandoned hands
or hands that stretch up vertical,
a motion almost of traction
and yet of not reaching their meaning,

they float palely to the ground
as they trail –
as they expand and tumble,
vaporous, attenuated trunks,
another forest walks among the trees
and drives another foliage.

A tunnel under the trees.
Dark grass, gravel:
a set of narrow-gauge lines, at daybreak.
The sun is coming now, steaming,
piercing the fogs at a lateral angle,
mute rumbling recurs,
metal in the grass sparkles,
morning sparkles,
till suddenly a hedge springs up
for the lines end there in the grass.
Beyond, just a few sleepers
like unsteady steps ahead –
on the clearing the sun stays.

Fore-noon. Great plants.
The great camomile meadow is still,
pieces of iron in it,
honeycomb density over it,
white-spoked plants the suns
white galaxy without waves and no wind.
Always. For ever. Noon.

[HM]

LÁSZLÓ NAGY

The Coalmen

In the outer suburbs the coalmen race their carts,
they forget the decorum proper to men of trade;
'G'd yup' they roar, and hoofs strike sparks from the dark,
'G'd yup', and the jolting cart-lamps leap and fade.

The carts are coaches! Their drunken, heroic burdens,
rolling and grabbing – hold in a splendour of black,
billow wraith-blooms of rum on the jangling air, –
dangling to watch the wheels, or lolling back

in a dog-tired daze, beyond the constellations,
with nothing above but the depths, the empty spaces;
they obey no law, they're numb to the tumbling hailstones
pocking like birdshot at their coal-grimed faces.

Steam flies, foam flicks! – the mighty, drenched dray-horses
thunder back to the stables, guided by instinct and desire;
but that Palace is far from lust for the dusty lads,
who will find sharp draughts, damp hay, and a guttering fire.

No wives await them, no girls that are game for fun
will wiggle wide hips and giggle behind the beams;
saltpetre will limn their lecherous lips all night,
the ammoniac stink of horses will plague their dreams.

Cold comfort for those who must lose the kind Kingdom of Booze, –
for such is their fate: even booze will be taken away.
So remember the lads on the carts; their rough-hewn hearts
deserve more than the coal-ash burned on a winter's day!

[TC/GG]

Squared by Walls

Couldn't you have died,
or at least bled,
instead of pacing the floor
stunned with despair?
You kept clear of the trouble –
bullets, armoured track, emblazoned
girls' screams. Nor for you broken
wheels, scattering rooftiles,
grim gangs of working lads,
and soot-brindled petals.
You did not spill one drop
of blood, and when it stopped,
you had only gone grey and mad.

In usual winter weather
you stand here; no other
but yourself, and wide awake,
squared by walls that echo
a cough like raking
gunfire. It's not merely
your flesh that's cold;
mind and heart are frozen, – crowned
by knives of ice.
You are ashamed of your melting phrases;
as if you had lost the right
to think of spring
and lilacs, – the lung-like trees blossoming.
What agony for a Lord of Life!
Yet, deep in the secret places
of your being, furtive with guilt,
you are breathing on the frosted pane,
that you may look out at the world again.

[TC/GG]

Cloud with a Woman's Face

I awake shuddering, a great pulse
banging inside me, a flame
flickering and jumping inside me,
and the world is burning around me –
up to the purple-trembling sky,
roaring fires of growth in the May sun.
Shine, shine, sun! drag shrieks
from the mouths of flowers as you force
them open! swish sap scalding
through stems and stalks! suck
out sweet leaves from close buds!
hoop growth-ring on growth-ring till
fat trunks burst apart!
Creation drunk on creation!
Foliage beckoning like a woman,
love swinging and ringing my heart
like a deep bell. A blaze, a daze,
a dazzle of glancing lights,
and I've lost all bearings,
I only know it's spring
raving of truth, beauty, love, –
the murderous, ancient themes
that take the breath away.
O May, May, I have learnt your law –
only a starving man may know you;
I've gone hungry for a thousand years
to understand your passion.
And I don't want ease and comfort!
The well-fed loll of pestilent shores,
where bright banners turn black
and the roses are worm-eaten.
It's life I cleave to! Slur of silks from flesh,
crackling hair in dark rooms,
nightingale-songs, and the din of flowers.
Enslave me with sweet music!
Let me sweat with pleasure!
I gather it all to no avail,
and I'm doomed to go on harvesting –
but this is the only life, and it's wonderful.

The flush of youth's gone; my flesh
droops and bulges, and still I cry,
May, May, your signs are good;
your sights and sounds are making me stronger;
inside me, and in my blue homeland,
a cloud moves, scented with olives –
a cloud with a woman's face.

[TC/GG]

The Visitors

They don't ring in advance, or engage in any
rituals of arrival. They come without ceremony, –

not waiting to be let in, either,
but entering through walls in a foggy slither

of becoming-bodies, naked, threatening: –
an anonymous company bent on some obscure reckoning.

They hang, they dangle in morning light,
their many-coloured flesh is rainbow bright:

blue like the electric storm of a meteor's fall,
map-blue like Lake Aral;

green like an April shower,
green like slippery naphta;

red like festivals, shame, rage,
bloodburning red like Dózsa in his fiery cage;

yellow like fields of feather-grass,
apocalyptic-yellow, like horsepiss.

I have known their kind for a millennium,
in love with a banner, in love with a drum –

too strong to be killed. My memories
abound with their resurrections. They rise

from fatal flayings, beautiful as ever, –
bleed them dry, you won't stop their heart's hammer!

What a morning! What disorders!
My house chock-full of alien visitors

who won't eat, smoke, sit still, or be gone;
who call me a lapdog in silent unison.

Their eyes are wolves' eyes, glowing, glowing,
and they mean to get me. I feel something pawing

at the mind that moves familiar thoughts.
My teeth are grinding stars! Fire floats

into my hair, star-fire sets it ablaze.
The rough pelt I have grown stiffens with ice.

My well-kept nails crook into iron claws,
and I howl with the pack, obedient to wolf-laws.

[TC/GG]

Love of the Scorching Wind
(to Margit)

Wind, O you wind who storms my blood
sigh of she-lion, sudden southerly
clash, you coppery-breasted brilliance
you buffet my eyes, you dance, you kiss; it's a distemper,
the green hill of my youth is yours forever,
I look back to where it is furrowed from your fire-passage,
guerilla wind, you stretched horizontal scream

sawing ribbon-silkily at my shoulder, fiddlestick
my veins' vibrator, playing my bones' membranes,
what orbiting star ordered you against me
to so fever-flood me, with restlessness fill me,
glaze my eyes with the wild lace of lightning, your voice
for which angry star does it pass sentence: 'There is no mercy,
there'll be no mercy'? – but serves me right, serves me right,
I chose to begin my life in your corrupting superstition!
here you are circling around my throat, chasing a tail,
phosphorescing with cyanide and arsenic fury, you've haltered me
          forever,
ah, my throat's your axis, you blurred disc aglow,
my wide collar of drought, plate spinning of hallucination –
full-blown with sacrifice you run amok in howling
intimidation for my raped early treasures, you bring wild-tasting
bunches of green love and kisses, my daybreak squeals in you,
so too the lamb of innocence, my chaste verse, gold hair,
my exorbitant foam, the sugared chain of my sins,
and in the middle my fool head – I'm singing for you,
whirlpool of whirlpools, wreath of Babylon sand stifling me,
you scorching, you yellow gypsy wind – you gypsy!
Stop now or slacken, I'd like to see my treasures!
All my happy years kick in a bundled foetal membrane,
I untie it with my mouth's strength, I sniff it nervously –
as a tired animal its litter – my jaw drops at my memories.
Blood and eyes are remembering faery light's leap,
the court of torments where lives a certain little king
at the world's centre in the sour-cherry tree, and wind
blows through it, a bell alive in passion's green-red tree –
that bell is I, both love and alarm
are booming in me, but no one hears, no one can see me –
look over here, dark girl! Only her necklace
throws flashing copper-coin suns in my face, she won't raise
her eyes from the cornflowers, though all the sanguine troop's
          asleep,
radiant the dreams of cowbell-hammerers, copper-kettle men,
they lie in the field all beard and hair, black nails in the grass,
the women dreaming too on their backs with bared breasts gaping,
springy hillocks where curly-haired babes are slithering
in milk and sugary spittle – oh, is there a God?
Look at me, dark girl! Only her helmet-pointed breasts are looking,
she binds herself with a cornflower wreath, with azure chains,

though the gypsy king in the tumbril snores bible-darkly
the tower of judgement's leaning, his unharnessed donkeys
and iron-shod hares are musing in the golden barley;
but blessings on the Moses neck over the tumbril's backboard,
let his keg-shaped head dangle, let the sun come between his
        snoring lips,
let the wind play over his thousand showing teeth, his hair
that touches the grass, and his wine-soured bubbling spit!

Come here, dark girl! She's standing, she's turning towards me,
small copper-oven hips tense and from between her thighs
– like a golden caption from a saint's ecstatic lips –
a miraculous bright ribbon issues. Don't be scared! I close my eyes.
Your wreath's nice. You're lovely. And like the wind, scorching.
My balls and everything burn like mad, my teeth are chattering
        for you,
I'll kneel for you, I'll use bad words – oh, this afternoon is but
damnation in disguise, a death's-head feathered bonnet!
Do you hear this row? Old bags and know-nothing virgins
rattle off a litany to Mary in the silk-snowed grove of flags.
Its noise makes me sweat; banners, tinkling little bells,
hateful bells coming to me through the cornfields;
you'll die you villain, snaps the priest, and the swords
sprout enormous and some swelling Hungarian kings ride
erect over me – oh, their curses befoul even my dreams!
Dark girl, you have left me. Your wreath's a dear blue-scaled snake
here on my numb asleep arm shivering as it dilates,
the long-haired tribe advances in the white dust down the highway,
and the scorching wind lets fall your song upon my sorrow.
Sitting on the yellow ramparts restless with desire for you
I hum awhile smoking myself into a stupor because of you;
by the time my fingers and lips ripen to gold you arrive,
I laugh and cry, what a fright! your poor little head's bald,
and you throw the bound sheaf of your hair at my feet bawling.
Who sheared my faery girl? Death – the song's 'old man death'
because she stole a small hand-mirror – 'that bloody old death',
caught by his dog, held by his son, that's how death sheared her.
I'll die if you cry: look, here's a little fleecy cloud
to drink your tears, from a smacking kiss your hair will grow again,
as for that old man with his son and dog, I'll castrate the lot
and add salt and red pepper seasoning; he won't shear any more
        faeries.

I sprinkle your dead hair upon the wind, there's a bird
to bear each strand into the blue air where they'll all sing sweetly
and a heaven of bird's-nests will rejoice at your gleaming hair.
Lion-maned faery, my blood's corridors are clanging from you
when the town's green belt begins to droop in the heat,
when towers everywhere sigh away colour and turn pale,
the tar-paper shanty roof gyrates like a leaf, and
emaciated horses are panting diamond-studded with flies
at the time of the wind when starred enamel flakes off
grass-overgrown thrown away pots and laths come away from fences,
at the time of wind and flame when a stray glimmer is enough
to pierce the violin to the heart and God's yo-yoing balls the larks
flying up and down shriek through superheated gullets,
and when I've fallen on my back and crickets chirr in my hair
and a blade of grass smokes between my teeth and catches fire,
for fire is waiting for fire and should not wait in vain:
then in a yellow skirt you step over my head, you delight, you
          mourning!
At the Grand Hotel B., I confess to the old waiter:
The wind of Balchik, grandpa, the Bulgarian Balchik
eats my blood, dries up my bones, but there's no mercy
nothing, neither refrigerator nor North Star protects,
and here is her letter of fire: If you are brave, you can come again!
Her message flickers with a yellow flame in my darkened room,
my eyes in vain contend with the blackmail of visions;
the last green crown is burning over the sandpit,
love consumes it at the stake of our two selves,
icons flush with fever, from the trees a glowing caravan
and a hundred Persian stallions from Dobrudzha run roaring
into the Black Sea to cool off – oh, what of me?
Before the gun-barrel gaze of the airport customs man I confess:
Yes, I took out with me a rose but brought only its ashes home.
I've arrived – what a place! What martial stone men,
a cold wind from every bored hole in their stone heads:
turning you to stone, turning you to stone, turning you to...
No! I shall not turn to stone, you stone faces; too bad, stones
for the scorching wind is my religion, I'm shouting for her through
          my tears,
with my fiery knife I'll fight against your frost, you moguls of stone.
Your smile sears me, come with my Streaky Haired Girl,
our singing shall be the scream of blood against stone,
I shall be good at suffering – fate killed the idyll,

but the scorching wind will walk me over the waters of horror
and razoring rocks even, for she marked me for herself long ago.
It's a miracle that the lightnings of your teeth
and dancing streaky hair can fit into this tiny rented room –
my suffocating delight! You are like the wind, scorching!
The best man whom we selected turned prematurely to stone,
your bridesmaid's lace dress is nothing but limestone,
we are marrying in your rose-embroidered blouse and my only
       shirt humbly,
it's nineteen fifty-two, our wedding banquet's a plate of sour black
       cherries
and breadcrusts our landlady set up on her kitchen cupboard to dry.
Your lips and eyebrows are writhing into my white shirt: first
       sickness
and your womb's fruit ripens at the golden trumpet call!
Wind, O you scorching wind guarding my grave,
you faithful bitch of mine – my faithful wolf rather,
who can the star be that created you to sit here at my head,
who sent you that I should have even here no rest?
Though no shred of my flesh remains, only bones, lonely
poor bones, thick hair and uncrumbable crown!
Wind, conjuring wonder wind, ushering prophecy,
it's you who will whisper, murmur, howl: Resurrection's here!
You are first to stand up, you kill off the damp
and the dark frost, you start digging the earth, you fiery
gypsy wind, you'd scratch up carrion even;
wind, you wild angel blowing your own soul into me
you set my crown on and drive me into Eden sword-flashingly
up the green grassy hill to meet every night with her
under the huge moon, she whom you've chosen for me,
so that the world should be stunned at each sunrise
to see blackened places on the glistening hillside:
Look there, where again Love was lying all last night!

[KMcR/GG]

LÁSZLÓ LATOR

Under a Heated Tin Roof

The silence, the sound, the fever, and the fear,
change places constantly, as if by chance,
some crater insists on disinterring here
her waste products of no significance,
their bubbles blend in depth and stratosphere
and all exist and all appear at once,
seeking emergence, form-autonomy
to break with death and death's monotony.

The warmth of rumpled feathers in the loft,
the lukewarm egg, the albumen and yolk,
a needleful of blood darkens the soft
vitellus in its circular blurred sac
of jelly. Exhausted pigeons brood and huff.
Life turns to its own heart and surges back
to find embodiment within a bed
of uterine heat where black is streaked with red.

Then seeds: pale scabs within a pit of wax
like mottled beans, where roughly tucked, a thin
ovule adheres precisely to a flux
of phosphor-and-lime in damp concretions
of swollen wheat, of rye's ribbed-fibrous husk,
red enamel of broomcorn-seed, peas blown
and fat, dim lentils, pearled millet, which endorse
their own peculiar inimitable laws.

Under a heated tin roof in the haze,
already squashy, and pulsing with the scent
of singed feathers and manure, with blaze
and throb of gashed tin, summer comes, the moment
of the predator's beak, the monomanic gaze
of an orbed eye aquiline and attent,
preparing to turn dagger and to mar
the perfect membrane with a jet-black scar.

[GSz]

When the Sooty Candles Have Guttered

When the sooty candles have guttered
to stumps along each migrant border
when endearments are fouled and scattered
their ranks reformed to a new order
when from a spinning dustcloud starlings
wheel in a body to a summons
from their place prematurely darkening
on the low six-o-clock horizon

when the mood of the drunken banquet
turns to croaking when premature wear
and tear start to show on the blanket
when morning goes about to prepare
a day that for you is more sombre
than those before and drily coughing
some conveyance melts in an amber
fog stinking of foul mash and stuffing

when stains that are just perceptible
and scales like barbs discover for us
qualities quite irredeemable
about our beautiful detritus
and form's whimsical capriccios
reveal the swift deterioration
of precise and delicate sketches
to sharpened powers of observation

when colour and light and its shadow
the taste the smell the moisture of matter
surrounded and hounded still follow
their usual round of endless chatter
when the trees stand petrified frozen
in their inflammable ecstasy
and when through the damp cleft the risen
tide swamps seeds in their maturity

when he is dissolved in his meagre
dream in his own warmth he listens
with his senses and instincts eager
to catch the sound of preparations
when enveloped in dreams the creature
in his own body's midnight senses
the mistaken pending appearance
of something like his death yet greater

[GSz]

The Meditations of Heraclius Gloss

How long have I been treading these galleries
big with illusions of reduced existence,
this dark so pitilessly circumscribed,
yet coruscating, bright with expectation?
If we assume the spirit's transmigration,
its rise and fall according to its merit,
and if at most the thing that remains hidden,
unseen by souls is that haphazard evil
of which they might perhaps have been convicted,
and the unit of eternal measurement
by which are weighed their actions in the balance,
if we assume the spirit's transmigration,
vast legions then, unmoving, march across
the impenetrable regions of our minds,
our uninhabited and common fate,
and all our memories are blocks of feldspar
grown transparent, or dull masses of slate
whose strata are compressed by a huge weight.
Whence otherwise those intermittent fountains
that spring to life obscure in shapes of dreams,
or else in one quite tangible clear-contoured
freshly-ejected part of some transaction?

Whence otherwise the underground explosions
and pit-gas combustions of anxiety,
the narrow fear that lives between our eyes,
the galloping thickets of our panic which
point to some lower fibre in our being?
Whence otherwise the brilliance and pleasure
of that moment when the walls cave in on us,
what current drives us then into the low
uncharted cavern of a musky night
flailed by the black hunger of the flesh?
Do I not feel how my thin skull is squeezed
and dented ever deeper by desire?

[GSz]

Abandoned Scene

The bird is sluggish, moving slowly
heavily lighting on the tree,
wind washes off what can be borne,
in circles, frayed, concentrically.

Smouldering on the hill's high crown
a brush-fire darkly billows smoke.
Some live thing singed by distant heat
recoils and beats a sharp retreat.

The scene's abandoned, tenantless.

No crumbling worlds stuck with pitted
swathes of clay, their tin-roofs slatted,
divided by enormous, skilless
hewn beams, mouldering and matted –

The soul has long migrated from
these rows of blistered walls and cast
her shape aside. Image and form,
the very circumstance is lost.

What is the source then of this light
which serves as sign, however slight
its message, persisting behind our lids.
Sometimes on an echoing night
the air wears faces like bright beads,

Drained faces in whose pleats the years
gather a rugged sediment,
which turn in dreams, within their blear
and suffocating element.

[GSz]

FERENC JUHÁSZ

Birth of the Foal

As May was opening the rosebuds,
elder and lilac beginning to bloom,
it was time for the mare to foal.
She'd rest herself, or hobble lazily

after the boy who sang as he led her
to pasture, wading through the meadowflowers.
They wandered back at dusk, bone-tired,
the moon perched on a blue shoulder of sky.

Then the mare lay down,
sweating and trembling, on her straw in the stable.
The drowsy, heavy-bellied cows
surrounded her, waiting, watching, snuffing.

Later, when even the hay slept
and the shaft of the Plough pointed south,
the foal was born. Hours the mare
spent licking the foal with its glue-blind eyes.

And the foal slept at her side,
a heap of feathers ripped from a bed.
Straw never spread as soft as this.
Milk or snow never slept like a foal.

Dawn bounced up in a bright red hat,
waved at the world and skipped away.
Up staggered the foal
its hooves were jelly-knots of foam.

Then day sniffed with its blue nose –
through the open stable window, and found them –
the foal nuzzling its mother,
velvet fumbling for her milk.

Then all the trees were talking at once,
chickens scrabbled in the yard,
like golden flowers
envy withered the last stars.

[DW]

November Elegy

My mind hunts in circles, sober, ruthless and cold.
The dull tapping of autumn rain numbs the soul.
Rain drips from the ivy leaves
in heavy, sticky threads: earth, sky, the roof-eaves
sweat with fever. Soon there'll be nothing alive!
I can't sleep, my mind has lost its wings.
My brain is a live coal, the bedclothes are flames
eating my bones. Ships' horns
cry from the Danube. The light from the street is sick,
it throws ghostly leaves on the wall, and tricks
the still, painted horses in my friend's
picture – whinneying, they dance from their frame.
I put my arm around you, your touch soothes me.
Under my hand your breathing is poetry,
pulse, rhythm, ebb, flow, the heart's knocking.
But sleep won't come, the rhythm's lame, and shies away –
the clear voice of sleep can't sing
my stunted dreams: of revolutions not fought,
memories, fevers, desires that swirl in the heart's
bottomless slush, churned by the killer hooves of contradictions.
My soul steams and smells like vegetation
after a sulphurous summer night of storms.
I get up, stand at the window: hollow, echoing sounds
from the town below, a baby's cry, an animal wailing.
Nightsmoke lies in the trees, reminding
me I am alone, how alone.
That sound I heard was the last tram flashing home
over the bridge, writing its sign in the rain.
And now, like someone slowly crossing the room,
a scythe taps on the wall... hallucinations!
I must lie down and rest. Sleep, so the nerves and brain
can heal. And the heart, the idiot heart.
My eyes burn, I can't sleep. And even if
    sleep comes, will tomorrow waken anything?

[DW]

Sorrow Bred to Perfection

Potato-bloom, potato-bloom,
fair sorrow, bred to perfection.

Numbness of my mother's garden,
potato-bloom, potato-bloom.

Behind parsley, dill, and verdant
poppy's slumber, potato-plant,

potato-bloom, potato-bloom,
mild sorrow, bred to perfection.

Paris, New York, I'd view their towers
but see instead your cell-born towers.

I'd watch the sea's fish sparkling
but see only your bloom foaming,

potato-bloom, potato-bloom,
gentle cousin, potato-bloom.

Below, where the purpling clay drains
into darkness, the bulging brains;

above shakes your flowered gloom,
potato-bloom, potato-bloom,

a faint wick-light guttering out,
green catafalque, potato-plant,

green love, making lilac-yellow
flesh-quivers for his love-arrow,

speaking to the envoys of space,
visiting ultra-violet rays.

Potato-bloom, potato-bloom,
you sorrow, bred to perfection,

you're no different from what I am,
the deathly hope of every man,

on this sea-bed's dried-out, well-kept
cultivated plot, wheel of light,

knot of women, all on one stem,
potato-plant, potato-bloom.

The same fluid that in you wells
up through your length, between your cells,

stirs the blissful animals, and
the inhuman grief of humans.

Exploding seeds, deep in soft flesh
bringing light, ascend with a rush,

and broodingly set floating free,
senses rebelling beautifully,

with the blood's hydraulic pressure
your being's glass-fragile structure.

Your deft mirrors, light-gathering,
understand hydrogen's exploding,

and transmit its detonation,
using the sun's self-destruction.

Ferny kisses, phase of quiet,
potato-bloom, potato-plant.

You too were the dream of the sea,
flower of my fidelity,

in you wheels up the perfect rose,
swaying, choked, stripped before it goes

hugging you, its one-eyed sister,
unconscious and impassive star.

I'd view London's iron bridges
but see instead your petals' arches.

You're no different from what I am,
the deathly hope of every man,

man's dreamed substantiality,
flower of my fidelity,

you sorrow, bred to perfection,
potato-bloom, potato-bloom.

[KMcR]

Seasons

Sped is Autumn! And decay is sped.
I tore towards you across the rotting plants.
My helpless eyes hid behind the vacant lids of the dead,
like solitary naked crabs in pearl-rimmed shells.
Dead men's shadows run purple from the whale-tooth railings.
Mouldering babies hang from their maw, and moaning soiled
chrysanthemums.
A blue dove they led towards me, her feet belled silver chains
trailing.
I slumped before your atom-splitting smile, turned grey under
your wandering glance.

And Winter's gone! Unlike others we knew.
The city's jaw of bells gnaws the bald heavens.
My teeth machine-gun the cold streets, where I begged bread
for you.
Winter ties up the woods in silence, knotting the white ends.
Hyacinth-blue the shadows from fairyland, behind that railing,
up to your silent window lope animals in a sorrowing throng.
Grey ruin hugging the lilac, at your bedside I listen to your
heedless babbling,
deer, hare, and thrush in the marked snow follow your flame-white
song.

Pitiless Spring! Foam encrusts the walls,
  organic green flesh has dried in a cracked glaze,
shreds of dead flowers shrivel beside spooled tendrils,
death's whirling arms for the bright seed grains reach from
    outer space.
Shadows vomit up green bile beside the railing,
cannibal sharks and saw-tooth starfish thrash hungry in swarms,
lust sprouts at your dribbled prayers, chuckles, and happy gabbling.
I throw myself here, grass on living grave, covering breasts fragrant
    as tombs.

And in time Summer! Into a gold medal it mints a people.
  The moon's randy stallion flashes his badge with a blue grin,
beneath ropes of nerves, cries of pain rise from the world.
In ultra-violet froth the insect slavers in its daydream.
Acid shadows are licking from the snake-fang railing,
lizard fingers grasp at your bulging heart, where many moths to
    red ash burned.
Under the hardening leaves, I listen to your female flower's husky
    moaning,
groaning by the red cave's dripstone garden, great panther, I, in
    your heart buried.

[KMcR]

from The Boy Changed into a Stag
Cries Out at the Gate of Secrets

Her own son the mother called
from afar crying,
her own son the mother called
from afar crying,
she went before the house from there calling,
her hair's full knot she loosed,
with it the dusk wove a dense quivering
veil, a precious cloak down to her ankles,
wove a stiff mantle, heavy-flaring,
a flag for the wind with ten black tassels
a shroud, the fire-stabbed blood-tainted dusk.

Her fingers she twined in the sharp tendrilled
stars, her face the moon's foam coated,
and on her own son she called shrilly
as once she called him, a small child,
she went before the house and talked to the wind,
with songbirds spoke, sending swiftly
words after the wild pairing geese,
to the shivering bullrushes,
to the potato-flower so silvery,
to the clench-balled bulls rooted so firmly,
to the well-shading fragrant sumach tree,
she spoke to the fish leaping at play,
to the mauve oil-rings afloat fleetingly:
   you birds and boughs, hear me
listen as I cry out,
   and listen, you fishes, you flowers
listen, for I speak to be heard,
   listen you glands of expanding soils
     you vibrant fins, astral-seeding parachutes,
   decelerate, you humming motors of the saps
   in the depths of the atom, screw down the whining taps,
     all metal-pelvised virgins, sheep alive under cotton
   listen as I cry out,
   for I'm crying out to my son!

Her own son the mother called
her cry ascending in a spiral,
within the gyre of the universe it rose,
her limbs flashing in the light rays
like the back of a fish slippery-scaled
or a roadside boil of salt or crystal.
Her own son the mother called:
come back, my own son, come back
   I call you, your own mother!
come back, my own son, come back
   I call you, your mild harbour,
come back, my own son, come back
   I call you, your cool fountain,
come back, my own son, come back
   I call you, your memory's teat,
come back, my own son, come back
   I call you, your withered tent,
come back, my own son, come back
   I call you, your almost sightless lamp.

Come back, my own son, for I'm blind in this world of sharp objects,
within yellow-green bruises my eyes are sinking, my brow contracts,
my thighs – my barked shins,
from all sides things rush at me like crazed wethers,
the gate, the post, the chair try their horns on me
doors slam upon me like drunken brawlers,
the perverse electricity shoots its current at me,
my flaking skin seeps blood – a bird's beak cracked with a stone,
    scissors swim out of reach like spider crabs all metal,
the matches are sparrows' feet, the pail swings back at me with its
        handle,
come back, my own son, come back
my legs no longer carry me like the young hind,
    vivid tumours pout on my feet
    gnarled tubers penetrate my purpling thighs,
on my toes grow bony structures,
    the fingers on my hands stiffen, already the flesh is shelly
scaling like slate from weathered geologic formations,
    every limb has served its time and sickens,
come back, my own son, come back,
    for I am no more as I was,
    I am gaunt with inner visions
    which flare from the stiffening hoary organs
    as on winter mornings an old cock's crowing
rings from a fence of shirts, hanging hard-frozen,
I call you, your own mother,
come back, my own son, come back,
to the unmanageable things bring a new order,
discipline the estranged objects, tame the knife,
    domesticate the comb,
for I am now but two gritty green eyes
glassy and weightless like the *libellula*
whose winged nape and dragon jaws, you know it well
    my son, hold so delicately
two crystal apples in his green-lit skull,
I am two staring eyes without a face
seeing all, now one with unearthly beings.
Come back, my own son, come back,
    with your fresh breath, set all to rights again.

In the far forest the lad heard,
at once he jerked up his head,
with his wide nostrils testing
the air, soft dewlaps pulsing
with veined ears pricked, harkening
alertly to those tones sobbing
as to a hunter's slimy tread,
or hot wisps curling from the bed
of young forest fires, when smoky
high woods start to whimper bluely.
He turned his head, no need to tell
him this was the voice he knew so well,
now by an agony he's seized,
fleece on his buttocks he perceives,
in his lean legs sees the proof
of strange marks left by each cleft hoof,
where lilies shine in forest pools
sees his low hairy-pursed buck-balls.
He pushes his way down to the lake
breasting the brittle willow brake,
rump slicked with foam, at each bound
he slops white froth on the hot ground,
his four black hooves tear out a path
through wild flowers wounded to death,
stamp a lizard into the mould
neck swollen, tail snapped, growing cold.
And when he reached the lake at last
into its moonlit surface glanced:
it holds the moon, beeches shaking,
and back at him a stag staring!
Only now thick hair does he see
covering all his slender body
hair over knees, thighs, the transverse
tasselled lips of his male purse,
his long skull had sprouted antlers
into bone leaves their bone boughs burst,
his face is furry to the chin
his nostrils are slit and slant in.
Against trees his great antlers knock,
veins knot in ropes along his neck,
madly he strains, prancing he tries
vainly to raise an answering cry,

only a stag's voice bells within
the new throat of this mother's son,
he drops a son's tears, paws the brink
to banish that lake-monster, sink
it down into the vortex sucking
fluid dark, where scintillating
little fish flash their flowery fins,
minute, bubble-eyed diamonds.
The ripples subside at last in the gloom,
but a stag still stands in the foam of that moon.

Now in his turn the boy cries back
    stretching up his belling neck,
now in his turn the boy calls back
    through his stag's throat, through the fog calling:
    mother, my mother
    I cannot go back,
    mother, my mother
    you must not lure me,
    mother, my mother
    my dear breeding nurse,
    mother, my mother
    sweet frothy fountain,
    safe arms that held me
    whose heavy breasts fed me
    my tent, shelter from frosts,
    mother, my mother
    seek not my coming,
    mother, my mother
    my frail silken stalk,
    mother, my mother
    bird with teeth of gold,
    mother, my mother,
    you must not lure me!
    If I should come home
    my horns would fell you,
    from horn to sharp horn
    I'd toss your body,
    if I should come home
    down I would roll you,
    tread your loose veiny
    breasts mangled by hooves,

I'd stab with unsheathed
horns, maul with my teeth,
tread in your womb even.
If I should come home
mother, my mother
I'd spill out your lungs
for blue flies buzzing round,
and the stars would stare down
into your flower-organs
which once did hold me,
with warmth of summer suns,
in shiny peace encased
where warmth never ceased,
as once cattle breathed
gently to warm Jesus.
Mother, my mother
do not summon me,
death would strike you down
in my shape's coming
if this son drew near.
Each branch of my antlers
is a gold filament,
each prong of my antlers
a winged candlestick,
each tine of my antlers
a catafalque candle,
each leaf of my antlers
a gold-laced altar.
Dead surely you'd fall
if you saw my grey antlers
soar into the sky
like the All Soul's Eve
candle-lit graveyard,
my head a stone tree
leafed with growing flame.
Mother, my mother
if I came near you
I would soon singe you
like straw, I would scorch
you to greasy black clay,
you'd flare like a torch
for I would roast you

to charred shreds of flesh.
Mother, my mother
do not summon me
for if I came home
I would devour you,
for if I came home
your bed I would ravage,
the flower garden
with my thousand-pronged
horns would I savage,
I'd chew through the trees
in the stag-torn groves,
drink dry the one well
in a single gulp,
if I should return
I'd fire your cottage...
and then I would run
to the old graveyard,
with my pointed soft
nose, with all four hooves
I'd root up my father,
with my teeth wrench off
his cracked coffin lid
and snuff his bones over!
Mother, my mother
do not lure me,
I cannot go back,
for if I came home
I'd bring your death surely.

[KMcR]

SÁNDOR KÁNYÁDI

I Shall Die

The way I die
will be such that even my last
gasp will be first
picked up then played back
on tape by
someone who re-
plays it a few times
toning it down till
it's more acceptable
or just wipes it
Better to leave him with
that hint of a smile
of course without bitterness
that's what he was like
with the hint of a smile
says that someone without
a sigh the someone whose stif-
ling hand I have felt
at my throat
through the whole of my wretched life

[CW/GG]

History Lesson

history – I tried to
explain it to the stones
they were silent

then I turned to the trees
the leaves kept nodding at me

then I tried the garden
it gave me a gentle smile

history consists
(it said) of four seasons
spring summer
autumn and winter

now winter is drawing near

[CW/GG]

Engraving

there are lands there is countryside
where though beautiful nothing thrives
but bitter burdock where in the eyes
of wretched people with harsh lives
a glimmer of pale hope appears
barely flickers then expires
hope that one day it will all be over
stares into space as if forever
black kerchiefs and black hats encase
each rigid parchment-yellow face
and like their own hands on their knees
just so they sit there stiff with unease
on those old benches which worm-eaten
have as their lives have ebbed gone rotten
they sit as if in engraved prints
of mexico or way up where once
on manicured vancouver lawns
I came upon those indians
day-dreaming in silence dazed
barely a flicker in their gaze
and hands resting on their thighs
our lives *their* lives
you travel far for a surprise
to shock like that how our eyes
are like those indians' eyes and look
more and more the way theirs look
as on a sunday when we've all
met for a quiet funeral

[CW/GG]

After-Midnight Language

there are regions where
in waiting rooms at night
as if a fire smouldered from
the stench's fumes and the half-lit air
a semi-nomadic after-midnight
language pitches its camp
groans and curses cleave the air and
gold-toothed and toothless horselaughs
climb the wall reach to the ceiling
stifle the outside shuntings and clatter
shoo the shocked engine whistles away
grow and swell nearly breaching the roof
from behind your cape you peep out anxiously
a vision of what's going to happen in let's say
two or three centuries haunts you
dangling their feet in the gothic window
of saint michael's church they toast each other
with the tabernacle chalice just as now
they bite off the caps of bottles
drink my gypsy brothers
and they drink and you peep out while
the booze gurgles and look for a handhold
no peter no matthew is witness only john
suddenly an infant shrieks then
with both hands grasps the swollen
exquisite spurting breast
it sucks as if it was booze grows huge
beneath your closed lashes the infant
is the big-headed shaggy voracious
christ of the after-midnight language

[GGo]

SÁNDOR CSOÓRI

Ague

What is this extraordinary crowding,
this seagull-torrent,
woman's screaming,
ocean-howling?
Trees collapse together
like men hit by sunstroke.
A moment ago I had a grape in my lips,
now I suck sea-ooze.
On my hand hare's blood,
frog-spawn,
silk of a night-gown are drying.
In a green coach of leaves, summer and my skull go driving.
Rain rouses me,
water stills me,
war in prospect hones the body –
Come on, I'll give even brave mouths my boot
if they hold me with their stupidity.
What is this, what is this rage, ague, change?
Poems go pounding through me like freight-trains.
Dispersed – my bones,
my vertebrae,
my brain.
My hand droops like a shot soldier
in trenches of alien beds –
Joyless fingers are busy about me,
with a blue sky they bandage me,
in the gauze of rivers they bind me,
and they carry me prone on the wind,
but where to, where?

[EM]

Barbarian Prayer

Wrinkled, unrelaxing stone,
rock of mother-daylight, take
me back again into your womb.
Being born was the first error;
the world was what I wanted to be:
lion and tree-root in one,
loving animal and laughing snow,
consciousness of the wind, of heights
pouring their dark ink-blot down –
and here I am cloud-foundered man,
king of a solitary way,
being of a cindery star,
and what I join within myself
splits me at once, because it goes
quickly and only sharpens yearning...
Wrinkled, unrelaxing stone,
rock of mother-daylight, I
stand at the entrance to your womb.

[EM]

Memory of Snow

At times winter changes its mind
and snow begins to fall,
in thick flakes, desperately,
as if frightened
that it won't see tomorrow.
It's best then to unplug the phone,
disconnect the door bell,
simmer wine with cloves,
leaf through letters from the past
and look back at my life
as if it hadn't happened.
As if no cannon had looked me in the eye,
no wanton eyes,

no worn hands ever reached for my hands
and everything that was politics, love
and the clamour of bells
would wait for me across the distance of an ocean.
It's best to imagine
that I could cry over my lost head;
the wind sweeps the lilac blooms over beds,
torsos and tousled pillows.
And I could stand at the last judgment
beside good friends, in a thin shirt, a light coat,
beyond smoke, taverns. Cemeteries.
I'd stare down a country
that is grandly debasing itself.
In my head the memory of snow;
snow, snow —
the plaster of a cathedral
peeling silently.

[NK]

Prophecy About Your Time

It will come,
you'll see, it will come,
before you begin to decay it will come,
the roughcast walls will feel the new morning down in their roots,
new summer,
a long day full of curtained groins and loins,
and water will soak through your canvas shirt,
your bones too will soak in water,
    swimming ahead,
        backward and upward,
as if you were rifling
the crypt of the sea —

it will come,
you'll see, it will come,
before you begin to decay it will come,
a pigeon will bleed as it swoops

and scrapes its belly on stones,
and the sky will be orange with the glow of conductor-wires,
and on heated boulevards
the cars,
          the words,
                    the cries will fly about
like pieces of lead shot, like caravans of lead,
and you will walk among them,
under cover
of smoke and of dust,
the invitation of death in the swaying of your body
but nobody will wound you then
because you've no memory,
and nobody will wound you then,
because you no longer live in your wounds –
Insanity! insanity! the mouths will hiss at you
like spouts in a gutter,
and under the sprinklers under their whiskers of water
so will the barnacled pavement –
Insanity! insanity! professional mannequins
with thousands of years of sickly-sweet smiles will flood you
and window-displays will show ants,
ants on the pavement in its grey basin,
ants on the barrack-squares of eyes left wide open,
ants in the clocks, in their beaten up works,
          coming
                    and going,
                              and seething,
they'll lay ceremonial
          wreaths of cogwheels
          on emptiness,
it'll be beautiful,
          I tell you, quite beautiful,
because only you can succeed in their place,
who knew how to wait
after the first pain for the succeeding pain,
to hide from red in the black
          and out of the black,
to find a daily embodiment,
to break out in sweat,
          to divide, to persist.

[GSz]

Confession to the City

How much rubbish the wind sweeps down the street,
how many faces drifting, emptied of matter
    and streaks of choking smoke below the city sky!
And how much bleached out love behind the walls!
But when the passions briefly change to green
    as signals do at traffic lights,
the branches which were restrained begin to sway, the rain
    descends from high in towering lacework curtains
and a brilliant madness shudders
    along the whole length of the tramway,
whistling and whining like a flute
    pitched at high falsetto.

I love you, I love you not...? For thirty years, city,
I have been tearing pages from your calendar.
    I amble down your streets
        with no idea of direction.
Here things lie close to hand and to the body,
closer to delight, to homicide.
The boilers are dragons who open monstrous throats
    to shoot their flames about my face, as in the legend,
and down below, under the crust, your sewers
    throb continuously in eternal squalor.
Am I yours then, city? or simply
    your prisoner?

Often I leave you, deny you and yearn to be where
even now the fire stretches out
    along the earth
        like some exhausted beast of burden,
and in gardens the hedgehogs scuttle, prehistoric representatives
whose velvety mumbling is suddenly rent
    by the squeal of your million windows, your fetters,
your lovely neurotic women who scream out forsaken,
and there I am with them again,
the lifts full of mirrors, shimmering upward,
    in the hair-raising draughts of the underground,

in multiple reflections from your million eyes and
from my own madness. If you will not accept me,
   only the woods may give thought to my presence, or death
      with his elbows propped on the moon,
and the world won't call on me in an emergency,
won't send for me, won't wait nor pursue me with music,
from which I may learn immortality. You tremble
   excitingly on my white membranes, like
beans on a drum in vibration. Does smoke swallow you up?
Earthquakes perhaps? Burgeoning roses of wildfire? Though I
     betray you
   I'll perish with you.

[GSz]

LÁSZLÓ MARSALL

An Old-Fashioned Request

Sometime, today in any case, relate to me
all the variations in your love for me,
from the first shudders of awakening
when the shards of last night's passion roll and sink
into the pillow still warm from where your neck
last touched it, each fleck crystalline, a sugar speck,
a micro-lens within which skulls, our own,
are tangled in a mess of dream-like down
a pinch of sun under the soffit of a gate
where seeing each other standing together we
fall asleep, for what's a pinch of luminosity
where the very brows of those who separate
throw such light below the soffit of the gate
where the shards of next day's lovemaking
a micro-lens within which skulls, our own,
are tangled in tomorrow night's dream-down,
while the pillow still warm from where your neck
next touches it, absorbs that sugar speck,
after your shudders of awakening
and variations in your love for me
that you will, today sometime, relate to me.

[GSz]

Solution to an Imagined Puzzle

If I were casually
to smash your skull now
and roll your brain out into a landscape
of necessarily reduced size
I would take fresh lime and burn to a frazzle whatever
hole might shelter some human rat's nest
– no one but me should inhabit you –
and on close examination with a magnifying glass
I should discover in wrinkles of the severally layered surface,

as in dried owl's vomit,
the indigestible fur and bones,
the packed and rearranged remains
of a hyperactive life,
could I bear even one more night
or a single hour
with these excavations, self ingested hecatombs;
or would I smash my own skull
and unroll my brain in much the same manner,
and discovering there in some fold or wrinkle
your remains,
and in them everything I had already found –
not knowing
if there at the very beginning, there even now:
whether this series of murders had a first cause:
or if it were endless?

[GSz]

...Amores Te Salutant

say it again: *I want to be yours* – and with closed eyes,
while I sit on the edge of your bed and lean over your face –
so what has happened so many times might rise and dance behind
          our eyelids
and have us observe our love-making selves;
that everything which has already happened should happen again
before the flesh-tremor comes upon us
roll your eiderdown to the wall as you used to,
so in that uncovering I might see many earlier uncoverings;
divest yourself, not of the lilac nightgown; flow from your black bra,
see the earlier hardenings of your nipples in the past of my lips,
my head sinking, the scattering of my hair
over your breasts that were; and let me see from as close as I can
          get, your nipples,
their aureoles my entire horizon; and feel again
the beating of my lashes against the hillocks of your breasts
while my hands work down your belly, and the tip of my middle
          finger gently

negotiates the dip of your navel – tight grip of elastic, scratchings
      of nylon, proceeding
from wrist down to my palm – as if stroking a day-old chick
so it runs past the softer lines of hair bisecting your belly, a thrill
      of dishevelment:
I speak in skin language you in furred groin language: I love you –
and now say it properly: *I love you* – and I hear that *I love you*
the quiet burr of the throat on the 'oo' at the end of the word in
      the depths of my ear
the tickling of your breath, my face having slipped from your breast
into the nest of my lips and the valley beyond your collarbone
      where I breathe:
– ⌣ ⌣ –, short hairs between my fingers and as your thighs part
my middle finger slipping into the salt steep chamber cleaving
      before it,
where a world of darkness, deeper, more spacious, scarlet pulsating,
with spirals of fire, opens its doors – and infinitely gently,
pianpiano I press the fishscaly key of an undersea organ
and hear the echoes, multiple reverberations
of your name my name, strengthening in my body, so in the centre
      of my groin
the names are already throbbing, and those *I love you*s,
said now twice over growing thicker more congested,
more stiffly more rigidly rising...
we too stare stiffly into the heart of that black scalding void
within each others' eyes, and only our past eyes note in the corners
      of our eyes
the soft choreography of our hands in undressing:
and the synchronised hesitant heartbeat that waits on the other,
which beats out the curve of our eyeballs; the Now of this mutual gaze
a terrible tyrant from whose flanks I see white eyed
the utmost white of your thighs, and the black triangular blindspot
      of fur,
and you can only steal a glance at what enters you;
and lying back is almost repose, and the falling-on-you,
breast-in-hand, the duration of a kiss, until the bodily tremor
      exceeding
the kiss within the kiss finds fulfilment in breast pressed
on breast, moving in circles, winding the humming top
in the blood as it spins towards the groins, and my hand sets out
from your breast to lodge under waist, under hips, in the warm dusk
between body and sheet, to raise those hips with ever more
      vehemence stroking

to the moment I breathe the word *mine* in your neck –
and again you repeat *I love you* in sea and tear-flavoured words
of blindly seeking curtains of flesh, spread thighs...
unsayable that eternal moment, when the I starting out of the I of
      myself
touches your fur, slides by and slowly, so slowly
your soft ring of flesh widens – o...o...o... you sigh
the moment of o...o...o...locked into those flesh rings, into my ear,
your delight is mine now: *I love you and in you*
still deeper, so you may fall fall into the first depth of bubbling
      scarlet
in the rhythm of that tightening and slackening, tightening and
      slackening,
and I see your mouth opening and your eyes beneath the lids
goggling into some mirror located beyond dreams,
so I may suck through my eyes the blind vision of your delight –
and the intenser blindness of your o...o...o...sighed into my breast:
a voiceless golden sobbing, for more and more within the within
      you...
and you speak my name to the rhythm of your groin as it grinds
      out its circles,
from a sea of deeper breathing, alerter for that,
locked into your thighs, with your furlips gripping and sliding over
that which in your labyrinths proceeds the message from me into
      you moving
like a ferry of flesh – and the walls call with their flood tide and
      flood gates
again and again and the o...o...slow preparation
swinging from black to red, and a death new born...
and again your opening mouth and under your lids
eyes staring into the mirror beyond death,
and I see ourselves above your face, from beneath your breast,
and the trembling of your thighs, and the thrusting of our groins,
      and
the single red eye of my groin sees the last wail of your womb:
the trembling of the tension of your thighs, the stiffening of your
      body,
my explosion juddering from nape through to soles,
the scarlet and white discharge into nothingness o...o
yourwithinmeness tumbling, tumbling, tumbling...

[GSz]

ELEMÉR HORVÁTH

The First Time

It was glorious to stay inside you,
you severe, green-eyed brunette
It was sublime that you brought me back to earth
that you spilled my blood
It didn't occur to me until now that there's death
The taste of immortality is salty
Kisses, July heat, blood, sweat flowing into my mouth
Thank you for pulling me back to earth
but paradoxically we ascended
This happened in a borrowed bed
in a shabby apartment
in a provincial capital
Thank you for not concealing your wrinkles
your warts and political convictions
We practically agree on things and I'm not young
What joy it is to love you through my senses!
To love you with your trimmed fingernails,
with your manicured short hair
You stand before me naked to your waist
wearing a hand-made skirt
You're a poetic patchwork
you formerly blonde virgin
I'm pleased that you're so harsh in your desires
in your egoism so naively soothing
I don't know how long I live
but I know that now you're the most beautiful
in this godly light
inside this purgatory
You smile you bleed

[NK]

A Chest with Painted Tulips

The soldiers burn down the village and they say
'this is victory'. Those who try to argue with them
are immediately shoved against the wall. Everybody
quietens down because they see there's no wall.
The child would love to bang the door shut
but there's no door. Instead, he turns around,
using his heels. This gesture changes his life.

Thirty years later he returns from New York
to take a picture of the ruins. He notices awe-
struck that all the houses have doors. On the threshold,
the doors turn on their heels; they may not want to
argue with him. The family is in the middle
of the room, painting tulips on a chest. A soldier
stands at the wall and fixes them with his gun.
The child would love to put a match to all this
but he's already old. He lacks the strength.

[NK]

Historic Winter

december 1956
wörgl in austria

there are frosted planks on a lorry
I load them on to a railway-truck at the station
and buy rilke's selected poems out of my wages

so as to warm me up

december 1992
sarajevo
r.l. a bosnian poet feeds a fire with his rilke

to keep from freezing to death

[CW/GG]

Orpheus Redivivus

He hadn't seen it yet but something
was burning something promised
all of Hades was burning
and the wings of the phoenix
the end-of-the-world baby chicks
the early within the late
and he surfaced to stop
the perpetuum mobile

The designated night held his attention
he didn't notice when the stamp of sandals
ebbed away he just kept kneading
the infinity of matter with the indifference of matter
until the strong light pierced his eye
and then beneath the burning beams
of the bush's blazing arch
like one who died and argues for his life

He has moved up out of dark
the blinding stones of constant night
in their stunning quest for life
past the forest's writhing dance
greening forth its final bloom
back up bravely into dust
snatches-of death-defying tunes
and of wretched cradle songs

man now bathed in perfect sunlight
as he sets himself on fire
becoming all-consuming light
he has moved up out of dark

In this glitter that poured on me
I see nothing but the sun
for seeing it in perfect night
blinded I am a perfect eye
have turned and others after me have turned
'Did you know him?' 'What did he do?' 'Where did he live?'
I am deaf I now have perfect hearing
a perfect tongue and I keep quiet

Love-dance now on razor-edge
of equal zero width and length
steps fleeting on a field of light
face vigilant on a field of light
waiting waiting at perfect noon
for stone and flower to burst forth
'I turned back and was too late'
now only silence which I hear I hear

[WJS]

GYÖRGY GÖMÖRI

Letter from a Declining Empire

Ever more frightening, ever more rapacious,
barbarian incursions are troubling
the Empire of Autumn.
And galloping on, the northerly wind
screeches through cloud-crevices, shears off
leafy crowns, tears down
beech-tree robes the colour of sealing-wax,
shedding their heavy blood,
cracking its whip at defencelessly shuddering maples –
and how the gold coins keep falling!
Down threadbare avenues, past gap-toothed palings
the raider's clattering by; he throws
a firebrand into a chestnut-tree, and whoosh!
leaves whirl and fly up into
an air-woven hoop of flame. There's no one by
to save the treasures, the infidel
can pillage unhindered, now only
the scattered watchtowers of silver fir are left standing.
And still the conquest is not complete. In vain
do frost-riders patrol down by the river,
in vain does the Khan exact ransom from the milder
October colours, from sky-blue and green;
the survivors learn how to live. Naked as
cornstalks rent and torn, and with earth's bitterness.
Once the marauders have cleared off, their savage
symbols will melt too trickling down the gardens, and then
of a sudden the new
but eternal year will rise and raise with sunshine a still more
            beautiful empire.

[CW/GG]

From a Traveller's Notebook

In Ruritania
there are no plugs in the baths
lavatory seats aren't sat upon but vomited over
offices smell of cabbage
culture of cheap eau de Cologne
With thickly padded shoulders in a jacket cut too straight
the writer stalks about in the field of Word
he bends down picks up a piece of reality
sniffs at it and chucks it away grimacing
he makes a bouquet of dew-drenched immortelles
for his fadeless merits
he shall while he lives be exalted
In Ruritania
the job of ceremonial incense-bearer
is not for everyone
only for those whose past *and* future
are equally beyond reproach
the dispensation of incense is important
though it does not make the task of post-perfuming
any less necessary
In the shops there is a crowd
for it is rumoured that a large consignment
of word-stock has arrived
words beginning with 'x' are on sale again
and there are 'z's galore (or so they say)
Oooh and if plugs should appear at last
sheets of sandpaper and pastry cutters
then in Ruritania
the deluge of satisfaction would shatter everything.

[CW/GG]

Abda

(in memory of Miklós Radnóti)

They made us dig. Leaden, grey,
the sky is empty of all but the beat –
exhausted, slow – of a rook's wings.
Carts over there, bored soldiers.
(How banal it is, the entire setting!)
And these aren't even Germans.
We speak the same language and yet the guard
can't understand a word I say.
The Book's prophecy and that of my own
prophetic soul are proving true.
The sponge is dipped in vinegar.
I pocket the little notebook now,
still inhaling the pasture's damp
and the brushwood smoke that wreathes the willows.
Non omnis moriar – yes I know
but now for the last time I can say *I am*:
I shall be a flame that soars in the broad sky,
a silent body laid in the damp earth.

[CW/GG]

My Manifold City

My manifold city, I summon up
your image through the lenses of the seasons.
Trudging to school (in short trousers)
down an alley white with hoar-frost, when
a small bird hops over a frozen puddle:
A-B-A-B, and look, I've got a poem.
Spring: riverside kisses drowned in sighs,
buds exploding in the Museum Gardens.
Then sultry summertime, on the Island roses
surrounding me with fragrance there, and love
is unexpected fireworks on Gellért Hill.
And finally – autumn, autumn. Winged songs
arching to clear skies, flapping flags
holed in the middle, the bright hopes machine-gunned,
and the darkly gaping hollows of ruined buildings
in heavy rain that blends all into grey.

[GG/CW]

LÁSZLÓ BERTÓK

At the Centre of the Universe

Whatever is event takes flight
though it pretends to stay behind,
we carry tables out to dine
the corridor is full of light

at the centre of the universe
as radiant as the sun we shine
our glasses raised but out of wine
this too is just a line of verse

reality and fact converse
within their common sphere of thought
but we ourselves prefer to shout
the real thing has the loudest voice

but no one's where he's meant to be
only the words in the glossary

[GSz]

I Run from Myself

You live more bravely, sealed up tight
a secret's a thing I hide within
but when sun blossoms on my skin
I tend to spill the beans outright

behind the skin-lock metaphor
stand creatures of sincerity
I run from myself once the key
has turned and I've unlocked each door

this is the ceremonial gift
I post on to you unaddressed
which you'll absolve once I've confessed
since life must go on, or must try,

and this excuse too must make shift
so you may catch me at the lie.

[GSz]

The Waste within the CNS

The will that binds, the vital juice
that is so quick to prompt the wit
the errors I may not commit
while once again all hell breaks loose

the moment grown into a word
when sensing my mortality
the acid in my cells, the free
galaxies enchained encurled

the slight bump and the shock delayed
the guilt in its brief blaze of light
divine salvation reason right
the loss of self the self mislaid

the waste within the CNS
the being myself nonetheless.

[GSz]

The Ladies of Bygone Days

Where with their magnetic breasts are Susanna and Martha
    and the Judys of various addresses
time has chewed to pulp Melinda and Vera and Liz my god we had
    breakfast with her bacon and eggs
Gisella what on earth was her last name gone too gone off on a
    Danube steamer
all I know about her is she was a company typist somewhere and
    she never heard of contraception till I told her and
then it was all amazement under blonde eyebrows and her Iseult-
    type blue headlights lit up
and I remember Eva too and her caveman-girlfriend the sculptress
    with her low forehead
and the gold-brown madness that looked for lasting messages among
    among the trembly lacework revives
its search in their Indian laps for New World treasures
    and the Copernican theory of their hips
over the Babylonian blind the legend ALBERT HECKLER MEN'S
    TAILOR sings out and our tongues incur damnation by the urgency
    of one unpostponable kiss
and what's Tonia that wild spinster doing in Paris and where are
    the adventuresses those Aggies and Cathys and Andreas taking
    buses to with their bursting shopping-bags
they have split dispersed gone without a message all over the stubble-
    field of civilisation
it makes no odds who did what the spicy details for instance whose
    husband it was dropped drunk from a New York taxi
they all live somewhere on the earth live well live poor no need to
    worry energy is conserved
where last year's snow was there's a green of this year's spring
dynasty marked for downfall youth crowned with arrogance the jacket
    taken out of pawn fitted your royal figure like a glove
ah spirit of heartrending elegies turn your noble eyes to Kertész Street
peeling plaster and whores and pensioners brought down in the world
G.T. the poet reeking of suntan-oil sported a newspaper in his breast-
    pocket for use as a flying carpet if the right moment came
and two true lovers merged into one body under a world-broad crackle
    of paper
while on the table Miguel Hernández was dying in a gaol of laurel-
    scented terza rimas

and his flashing bones made lightning in the room and lit up the
    legend tacked to the wall A FRIEND'S FLAT IS NO BROTHEL
and apocalyptic whimpers stole out from the freedom-flavoured stench
on the undying day of the faceless watches when language had still
    to invent the future tense
where the mother of two tempered by shivering fever-fits with a jug
    of milk in her hand cycles smash into a lorry
and the three-dimension-clasping limbs are crushed flat into the sheet
    of an asphalt-album scrawled with skid-marks
in happy mother's present time the green blades of the earth besieged
    the world's ice
and the scarlet of Viking lips swam on the shoreless sea of a cushion
and the bodiless starpelt panther lolled and clanked in its planet-kennel
    retracting its workaday claws
Downy creatures dusty earth-chicks your firm flesh and your elegance
the tongues chirping with 'I says' and 'I don't want none'
but I plan to live forever on a dilapidated iron bed admiring the
expertise of your professor fingers
with you away sky and memory shiver shudder bleak
but strolling the world on the leash of your arms among the machine-
    gunpitted walls was wonderful
wrinkling at the grave my nose picked up immortal scent from the
    embers of your bodies
I watched my enchanted ones grunt over the mud of bombs in the
    besieged sty
and the wartime Circe had neither chiton nor curls of a goddess
    and Greek urn-figures were not her style
nothing is more perilously beautiful than the live mines of your laps
the history of your hair whispers pleasure in this bomb-crater rolling
    round the sun
the spinning wheel of fate has threaded your arms about my vertebrae
    for good
to step from the burning bush of your slips you mutter to me and it's
    hoarse GIVE ME A LIGHT
while our shivering cells devour each other in a sweat of honey
and embers of spring of creation-the-destroyer hiss through our fingers.

[EM]

The Father of the People

Which monarch–cum–deity had fewer restraints or more power?
His was the way, the truth and the life, but chiefly the death;
his world was as simple as Russian Roulette,
the red ball, obedience: the black, execution...
A brief generation, to see his fallen statues' living original –
the short-assed, vengeful, industrious genius of organisation,
who dickered with his penknife in a functioning watch,
but failed to grasp the ideal in whose name he murdered.
Divinity requires a godlike imagination,
a pinch of poetry to go with the hard-line of strategy –
conscience and soul are not merely words in a spectrum,
sooner or later the lie starts to rot in the firm-looking binding,
and chronically sneezing, time, the monumental mason, carves on the
            tombstone
of common memory: Xerxes; Capone; the once fearful name of the
            emperor.

[GSz]

A Roman Considers the Christians

May the gods forgive me but I really can't abide them.
Their idea is a great one, but look at them all:
a bunch of quarrelsome eggheads picking their noses,
who, under the spell of their thesis, would if they could
be hard-line dictators, all for the sake of tolerance naturally,
who'd not kill with weapons but with murderous disdain,
while breeding their own sloppy aristocracy,
along with other oppressive, life-hating state institutions...
So, let me embellish this with a gesture – a fig for them all!
Just one little problem: the starved lion bawling in the arena...

There are plenty with vision, but they are the ones prepared to be
    eaten
in dust clouds of water–cannon, where out of the screaming and
    bloodshed
something emerges... the same thing? the worse? or the better?
the gods only know, if they know, what lies in the future...

[GSz]

The Spirit of the Age

I saw a beggar. Recognised him. Knew him instinctively. 'You have
a damned nerve,' I cried and shook his shoulders in cold fury. 'You
dare to poke your nose in here! Aren't you the liar who told us this
would be positively the last struggle? Wasn't it you who promised
every poet a redhead or red way ahead – to each according to his
need?' I stood there for a long time screaming furiously... eventually
he raised his hooded head and I saw he had no eyes. His hollow
sockets were a keyhole opening on to a smooth and endless plain
where fire and smoke mingled, and invisible feet pounded over a
few exposed bones. It might have been cavalry or fugitives. There
was the dreadful constant sound of something grinding. I couldn't
tell whether it was a loose axle or a human cry, or if it was the earth
scratching its bloody surface in the eternal drought that follows
tears of suffering. Then he addressed me in a flat exhausted voice
as if talking down a microphone. 'You think yourself a seer because
you've been disappointed. And in your infinite wisdom you bawl at
me like some cheap whore. You come back with your dowry, your
naive ideas, your bloody revolution! Bring back God, the family,
tradition, and kick me out! But are we not one person? And isn't
your imagination the whole problem? The wheel of time remains
indifferent, you are the squirrel in the cage rushing round on the
wheel which like a lathe turns out the centuries.' He fell quiet and
the wind dispersed him and nothing remained of him except the
cooling ground where he had sat, and fire and smoke and dust.

[GSz]

A Nice Little War

Of course a war would quickly solve our problems; Behemoth would answer: no more bald heads, no more surplus value, no New Left, no question of sex, no community projects...The fever of youth could take a cold bath. Or one of fire. Why not? Imagine! the sea of swollen flame would stop before the cellar stairs. Imagine! those who have nothing would not be ruined by their losses...it would be their turn at last...the southern hemisphere would remain...Brasilia ...this way madness lies. And not just because of the flattened steelworks or the mountains of corpses. We sought god and found ourselves; our limits; I am as I am because ultimately I cannot be anyone else. A clean sheet then? Inscribed with blood? If one could lean over the balcony of the stars this perhaps would prove our masterpiece: the pattern that dictates the passing of time. However, excessive objectivity disgusts me. It is precisely the smell of the earth that is divine in me; those I saw ploughing with wooden shares and tractors; the taut ocean begins to hum, and round it the reference points of the face of infinity...trees, pot-holes along the road, a centipede...as far as the world is concerned poetry is a matter of detail. I learned this during the storming of a city, the lesson took less than half an hour. At first we heard only the breathing. The wheezing of an enormous pair of lungs some distance off. Then we understood it was our lack of air pumping the live bellows in our chests. A vast silence followed. The sense of dizziness at having survived. An iron door. A gallery above. Mortar between clumsy stones. Later the silent film: coats covered in brick dust swaying at the resurrection ball...eyes drinking light like lidless mirrors... Could I look into another mirror now? The conquest of the world left me behind to act as messenger. The news burned up my lips as they were muttering: NO.

[GSz]

A Visit to Room 104

I saw how death pursued its calling in peacetime;
carving fine detail, a vigilant minor craftsman:
one lump on the thighbone, one on the brain, one by the eyes –
he worked in fine temper and whistled a tune down the oxygen tube...
All our lives we prepare for the great Titus Dugovich scene
where we perform a spectacular double-twist dive off the castle
            ramparts
and make an impression on our descendants –
a downbeat ending comes as a surprise...
We're not prepared for the fact that our bodies pack up –
that we find no space in bed for our hands or our legs,
that we spend the whole night on a bed of sharp nails, tossing and
            turning...
mud then or spirit? The choice of the romantic,
of the archer with one eye shut, of the eschatologist –
from death's point of view all things are mud, even the spirit.

[GSz]

DOMOKOS SZILÁGYI

Beethoven

A deaf man playing music to a deaf age –
heard at a distance of 200 years.

People, if there's anyone among you
able to hear the music of deaf epochs –
stop your ears, like Odysseus, with wax!
Yes, that would have to be your unconditioned reflex:
bound to your own epoch as he was to the mast,
for, oh, what would become of the world,
what would the world turn into if we had the courage to foretell its fate?

I am listening to music that goes back 200 years.
I am listening to prophecies.
And woe unto me a hundred times: that my past was foretold so
        long before my birth!

                    *   *   *

The concert hall grows larger.
It's always, when space expands, a little lonelier.

Herr Beethoven, conductor: can't you hear how mankind is singing
        a *different* tune?

The conductor is reprimanded and walks out,
though he shouldn't have believed what he was told!

No change. Now in silence and an everyday manner
lying to one another, sincere in their shared faith,
they gather in this hall, all whom this deaf musician
teaches to hear.

[CW/GG]

Frontiers

I keep coming up against frontiers,
always frontiers.
Things *on this side*, attainable things,
end up hurting me. The urge
to learn what's there, *on the other side*, hurts too.
Also I lie that I'll learn how awaiting me
there at the frontier
is the sacred lie: which is hope.
It waits, I wait – we all wait
here at the frontier.
The frontiers expand and I follow them.
I set out on my journey – they expand
and thereby become impossible to cross.
In this way I get richer all the time,
and the richer the greedier.
I keep walking along the frontiers;
I lie all the time –
lie to myself, to you,
to everyone –
that I shall cross them and bring along
the Earth as my sad baggage –
there'll be duty to pay, for there, there's a frontier
and half my baggage they won't let through,
the half that is murderous,
the mad half, the hypocritical half, the half
with morbid spots like a corpse's, the deathful half,
stone-cold, that weeps tears of snow.
And yes, there will be a divorce:
the lie will divorce hope
after a marriage of a million years,
and until then,
till then I shall walk along frontiers, trudging along,
and the lighter the baggage that I cross them with,
the deeper the prints I shall leave there in the ground.

[CW/GG]

Job

(a statue by Mestrović)

All skin and bone, an old Jew, fit to die,
howls from this dust-heap earth at the cold sky.
According to His will, the Lord up there
has used and done for him: now Father dear,
now wicked urchin – whether bad or good
depends entirely on his changing mood.
All skin and bone, an old Jew, fit to die,
howls from this dust-heap earth at the cold sky:
'Naked, oh Lord, orphaned and poor I've stayed
that You might never lose the bet You made
with Satan – not on my account – that he
'd go green to witness such deep loyalty.
Whatever by caprice You chose to take –
three daughters, seven sons – I for Your sake
have laid before You, Lord, with my livestock –
asses, camels, every herd and flock.
But this is all mere air – nothing to me.
I ask no greater favour than to be
a beggar, Lord. Let me be plagued by lice,
let rampant sores consume me, and may this
seem so much more than a good job well done
that in the end you'll say: "Good Job, good son,
enough: there's no one of more trust and worth
than My true servant Job throughout the earth.
His flock is scattered, every beast is dead,
there is a dust-heap where he laid his head
and poverty is now his bedfellow,
making him of all beggars there below
the wretchedest...Come, angel, the good Lord
must see His Job's prosperity restored –
which Job once lost in answer to My voice.
Now he will get three girls and seven boys,
a burgeoning harvest and a mighty herd,
long life and power with it. This is My word."'

Then saith Job: 'Lord, rejoice, as you may well,
but not to wipe out all that once befell.
One suffered. Was that nothing? It can't be so.
What does it matter if, adoring You,
I live four generations, always well
acquainted with Your mercy, and of all
those days no day is spent in weeds and dung?
But however much I am, by old or young,
loved and respected, no, no one can be –
not even You – Lord over memory.
For during sleepless nights, my grandchildren
will still remember as they toss and turn,
and feverish with horror they will cry
howling from beds of flame at the cold sky.'

[CW/GG]

ZSUZSA TAKÁCS

The Double

My worst recurring nightmare after our separation
was that I would see you at a table
outside a cheap café in the Octagon,
every time I left my students and walked home
I'd see you lounging there where in return
for some piffling favour they would buy you
a scone or a cheese roll.
Each time my heart stopped still:
the same physique, same shape of head and beard,
and – don't be angry – the same slightly
down-and-out posture, have they been starving you
or are you begging for love?
and all the time you're wearing this horny expression.
I imagined it was you,
and forced myself to miss the bus,
watched you in secret, frightened of course
that I'd draw attention to myself by my behaviour,
that this other would misunderstand me,
since he surely wouldn't believe why I was doing this,
I'd be pleased to get away with
no worse than paying for his scone, or rather, yours,
since I spoke of him to myself in the second person.
But my fear was groundless,
for he never noticed me, or rather, you didn't,
and I was tortured by the thought I was no longer
attractive to men such as you,
it deeply wounded my self-respect.
And while I was thinking all this, you got into such
an awful situation, I almost cried out,
you had been given a slip of paper
and were to take it to the photo shop next door,
there must have been something bad written on it
for if the girl behind the counter refused you
you would be beaten up, and if she didn't
she would join the rank of your torturers;
but you must clearly have been hoping
that if you returned out of breath, you could
take your place among the card-players again

and though you had lost all your money
they'd give you credit (I also recognised
your passion for gambling).
So you waited for the note,
the first time they handed it down to you
from a height, then suddenly snatched it back
and dangled it under the table between the table legs,
and you made several grabs at it,
just like a dog after a bone, I was already
feeling ill, and you laughed willingly; your laughter
lashed me like a whip; it was how you used
to laugh at some sophisticated joke.
Meantime the spectators had changed about,
buses were coming and going.
Soon you had finished your errand
and returned with money. I recognised
neither your stained suit, nor your exotic tie
which showed monkeys swinging from a tree.
It would be an exaggeration to say I was crying
but I wept bitterly in my heart.
It was my cousin who disturbed this fantasy,
thinking I was waiting for a bus, not knowing
I was saying a final goodbye to you.
We got on the bus together and she asked me
what had happened. I said, my students had died,
it was my last journey on this route, it is autumn,
the trees are rotting, do I need to make myself clearer,
the gravestones are toppling,
no, she said, she understood.

[GSz]

The Perennial Lament

There will be those among you who will not be able to look
at a woman again, the mere look of the wound, the smell,
if you survive it at all, will be enough,
the need to repeat the act will forestall you,
the broken spines, the sobbing which turns
suddenly to a scream you will hear
as if it had a will of its own.
Oh that perennial lament!
Beg to report, we have ripped off her shirt!
Beg to report, we have thrown her on the ground!
She was wailing like a broken siren.
Beg to report we made her lie on the door we smashed down
because she tried to escape. Beg to report
We could see she was old. We saw she was ill.
We saw she was a child. Beg to report,
we had earned the special permit,
each and every one who was there!
But the worst thing will be to do it again,
to go into battle for the sake of a woman.
To fire and to take the objective,
and then to hear something whispering:
No witnesses now! And palms sliding over
the open mouth of a cry.
Whatever you want, my love, but no screaming!
Whatever you want, only cover yourself,
from now on please wait for me
in a darkened room! Beg to report,
we have thrown her on the ground and have raped her!
Beg to report I threw her on the ground and raped her!

[GSz]

Refurbishment

Some slips and vests, some sticky blouses, jumpers
shrunk or stretched, that prickly woollen
waistcoat, a lot of unwanted stuff
picked up at sales, that skirt too easily creased,
soaked walking boots in which
my cracked heel bled,
paper tissues in a chequered pocket,
blown pages of Updike dropped in the bath,
inkstain, greasestain, heartstains
on discarded rags. 'A prosodic approach to the translation
of Lorca' offprinted in eighty-seven copies.
A white tie mourning with a dirty edge.
Second rate authors, duplicate copies, prescriptions not collected,
an empty notebook with the word DIARY
silver-embossed on the cover, children's bathing towels,
a one-week luncheon voucher dated seventy three
(every day I dined with someone else),
a dried ink cartridge, in which
is written the terrible truth:
arrivederci, youth.
                    I'm sitting by the open doors
of the wardrobe while workmen rip
the house apart and twenty years spin past.
The inflatable paddling pool, now patched and mended,
the Italian gymslip which fitted years ago.
and a hospital report (ab. incompl.) discovered
in the silk pocket of a sun bleached denim handbag.
My brows cloud thinking of that May morning.
                    Clods of earth tumble
like plaster in the renovated flat.
I sit inside myself, picking at musty grapes
of autumns past.
I hear the neighbours come, but no one
crosses the mountain of rubble. Dust flies, creeps
under doors. Once I feared cockroaches:
their thousand feet no longer frighten me.
I manage among the sounds of demolition.
Clothes unmade and yet already ruined
flap on the clothesline of the future.

I writhe in sweaty man-made fibres and sandals.
I laugh at undeveloped rolls of film
with ever greater abandon.
Hoarded addresses, unrecognised telephone numbers
bulge in tomorrow's diary which slips behind
a drawer and can't be found,
only paper bubbling from jammed drawers
I've tried to force open.
So we have been dwarfs in Lilliput –
Why should eternity care about that?
– It's only our lives.
      With one hand we grope about
our sentimental hearts. Our laced up feet, like Magritte shoes,
wait for permission to enter the secret gate.
Our eyes, cracked with use, drop the odd stone
or tear on buttoned uncomplaining lips.
Wrinkled necks of silk hiss in a fresh gust of wind.
A lacy breast sags light as a butterfly
across an ancient bony shoulder. Once blood
was fire in a bottle of scent.
I could start over again, writes the
hand, slowly drowning, on the sunworn horizon
of a fading shore.
      The day was long ago.
      I might forgive you –
If non-existence were possible
Interred in such rich soil.

[GSz]

DEZSŐ TANDORI

The Belated Halt, or Dr Jekyll's Dream

Mersault, then Murphy. These are important stations.
We clackety-clack right through them. Now Oran,
and now, Hyde Park. We throw cold water on
some lively arms waving at their relations,

(a daring image) or friends trapped on the train.
Then they depart, the people at the turnstile:
they know what's transient, and what remains.
It is quite clear, their guests coming by rail

have not arrived. Precisely: the train didn't stop.
Our boring expectations turn to nameless
excitements: But what about *me*?... my home?... my shop?

Which aren't the questions. Soon we cease to fault
our insulation from the "factual" world.
(With squealing brakes the train begins to halt!)

[TC]

For the Klee-Milne Sketchbook

Let us set out into a charming landscape.
We're pleased enough; we don't want other kinds.
A rhyme is coming shortly, and a shape
(or shapes) not novel: often on our minds.

Where are we going. Do I have to say?
We've had a jolt already, at the ford
across the river, or the waterway –
that dull white strip dividing words from words.

We amble onwards with our gentle friends.
Signposts emerge: we note them as we pass –
our bears beside us on the road that wends

...where to? We've just begun, and round this bend
now turned, we see our pleasant journey was
a rambling preparation for *The End*.

[TC]

Camille Pissarro
Rue d'Amsterdam, 1897

Rue d'Amsterdam is awash with rain.
Meanwhile, as if the sun shone bright,
the ankle-deep water is bathed in light.
Through the house-walls' multi-coloured stains
a radiance, hidden by plaster, penetrates.
Now the rain washes away,
pugs the surface into a gray
clay-like plasticine state.

I'd love to live there in eternal rain
if I could only believe the paintings, Mr P.
I'd be most happy to wave if only
an open yellow-red cabriolet
drove by – though I'd end up that much wetter
the longer I stayed there waving in
Rue d'Amsterdam, bathing in
the cool inner stream of light-filled water.

If I knew that I really *had* a cache
of radiance, only hidden by
some substance from whose surface I
could on the spot be freed by a splash
of pouring rain – if that's what it took,
I'd step out into the rain forthwith
as long as it rained on me just like this.
But it will stop. I close the book.

[DT/BB]

Utrillo: 'La Belle Gabrielle'

He was not left completely alone. Red.
There stood beside him, green, the good-hearted
innkeepers. Grey. Uncle Gay, the 'Casse-
Croûte''s owner, yellowish-violet, and Marie
Vizier, the proprietor of 'La Belle
Gabrielle'. Blue, black. They both
loved the eccentric, soberly decent and
childlike painter. Olive-green. When
he was alone, white, and didn't feel like
painting or drinking, sherry-colour, he played
with a teddy bear and a toy railway. Prussian
blue. He spent most of his time in the back
room of one or the other of the two inns. Brown.
He didn't go out to paint; azure and orange;
he knew if he went into the street, sooner or later
he'd have one too many, pink, would pick a quarrel
with the passers-by, greenish-white, and at such times
it was always he who came in second. Black. He
bought picture postcards and carefully en-
larged them. Yellow, reddish-purple, green.
Since, white, olive-brown, he hadn't received a thorough
training, he couldn't paint 'from memory', carmine;
he needed the sight, orange – the picture postcard. The
colours, however – red, grey, green,
black, white, brown, yellow, orange-red,
reddish-purple, and so on – he himself superimposed
on the grey, white, blue, carmine photograph.

[BB]

An Otherwise Unoccupied Swimming Pool in 1965;
A String of Similes

As if in an unoccupied swimming pool where only
maintenance men, mechanics, street sweepers,
idle ticket collectors, snack bar attendants hang out,
only office underlings, possibly
the management itself; and one or two amateurs like me
who got there who knows how and who
don't talk to each other, at best we're collectively
objects of indifference to the specialist staff,
bored as it is even with the professionals; as if
all alone in the morning at the deep-water end of
such an unoccupied practice pool, I were practising
the racing dive, something I've been
unable to master for nearly thirty years.
And so it's as if this wouldn't be me,
as if I'd consequently be practising with somebody,
so I'm again and again for a moment completely
alone, as among sycamore leaves and a tide of
spittle, other insignificant filth,
chucked-up bugs, my head pops up after
one of a number of by now perhaps not
entirely unsuccessful dives; but quality
won't cut any ice here, besides the whole thing's
just a string of similes. As if someone
would want to repudiate existence, but I'd
be insisting, as a father taking his such-and-such
son to practice the racing dive. Or other things.

[BB]

ISTVÁN BELLA

The Nights of O.E. Mandelstam

1

White white white white
white white white white
white white white white

2

Who planted a blackbird in my throat?
Whose will ordained a razor-blade nest
in my throat, lined with birdwhistle pipes,
a knife-flashing revel lasting till death?

3

It's a chain I pluck, not a lute;

my vocal chords clatter like chains,
or like the stars up there,
those worlds shackled with iron and gravity,
planets-in-fetters,
                        like my heart.

4

Oh infinity – Siberia of the world,
my blindfold pillory...

5

Snow
        is the moon
                of winter

6

I, the only begotten son
of the Jew, leather-merchant from Petersburg,
                        I who was born a tree
why am I now stone, night hewn from a block of stone.

7

And I shall teach human speech
to the againwords, to the songyearning trees,
I shall teach sky to the birds...

8

My whisper is an infallible leaf,
its sprouts leaves leaflessly, though mouldering
dead leaf-mould is all, all the shadows behind me,
and I sink onto my back as into rich leaf-mould –
back into my shadow, myself only shadows
– and yet I am: word before lips,
leaf-rustle leafless and treeless,
I am *to walk*, before feet, before wheel,
I am the future tense of *without*...

9

(See how moon-helmeted the night stands guard.
It inscapes from inward me, it grafts me upon me.
Its face gleams
and grins.)

10

Good God! My eyes are a home for bats.
My eyelashes hang
feet downwards
like nightitude itself.
At least give me
back the gallows
of the sun!
Light! light!

11

White white white white
white white white white
white white white white

12

In a filthy old coat as in a velvet cape,
with my red hair as under a crown,
'General! General!' – shout the children
in the street, so I stop.
They are my decorations, their smiles
my epaulettes, their hands my sword,
their births my future
medals.

13

Candles, and candle-poplars are ablaze,
my poems stuffed down my throat are ablaze,
my whitepaper mornings are turning into soot,
ash-flakes of silence writhing into soot.

– The writing burns blackly, like blood.

14

It soughs white, like a face out of silence.
White white white white

15

'When I wrote this, the sky was clear.'

[GG/RB]

Instead of a Letter

Raining again, again my heart
is merely a blue-green mess of bruises,
again
I am drenched in your red, green, yellow neons
Warsaw
and Budapest;
Who'd have thought you'd have grown grey like my hair
like the rain,
like wind in the trees,
who'd have thought it?
Here you are every crumbling wall,
each flickering nightlight, each glowing
salute of roses,
you are every new house
and each new storey.
I press your hair to my face but the wind is slack,
it slips betwen my fingers,
and nothing remains but the sky in retreat,
and my heart which grows heavier,
between you, between me,
between earth and sky,
leaping without a parachute
in free fall.

[GSz]

Prologue to My Poems

I brought back stones from Siberia, the bark
of a birch tree and some exiled buds
pressed into a book: words disembarked
from snowy wastes, and only the cooling body
of flowers linked by winter left some
frost-stained writing behind...

                    But though your words become
a struggle for breath, it was never the world itself
you wished to write: tree-for-tree, flame-for-flame,
the impossible, forbidden, self's own lack of self.

I'd write, on a birch bark too, if such a thing
were possible. As convicts do. How happy I might
be if my poems turned into poplars, surviving
the winter, each leaf a cell of living light.
Each refers to its ancestry, the human event,
and then beyond it to that one-in-a-million
singularity – me, you, itself – the accident
of now, of life and death and love now, which goes on
breathing its infinity into the present.

I've been there. Under sky. Walking on the ground.
Search hard for it. Don't leave it disinterred.
But it gave no sign of wanting to be found.
Nor clod nor sod responded, nothing stirred.
A shower of silence, sunlight. Above me, sand
whirled in air, yarn yellow as the sun. Around
me lay the taiga. Dumb. Green-prickly to the hand.
Like barracks in a threatening surge of sound.

After this I loved only my poplars.
October trees. Their skeletal solitude.
Their dry smiles and lipless whispered rumours.
Their autumnal branches, leafless and denuded.
I'll clutch their bones, they shall be my study.
It will be as though I had embraced my father's body
underground. Time turns to dust. Mills: unmerciful
bonds, blackbirds have leased my skull.

What I'd like is to have words for nothing,
for everything to be an I. For silence –
if there's silence – to be a soundless ringing
and its clappers an earthshaking resonance,
the heart too ringing, eternity-replete
in mankind's night, earth-sky a burning brand.

Throw this poem away, friend. Hold it in your hand
and see it smoke, then catch fire, the whole sheet.

[GSz]

GYÖRGY PETRI

By an Unknown Poet from Eastern Europe, 1955

It's fading,
            like the two flags that, year by year,
we'd put out for public holidays
in the iron sheaths stuck over the gate –
like them the world's looking pale, it's fading now.

Where have they gone, the days of pomp and cheer?

Smothered with dust
in the warmth
of an attic room,
a world dismantled holds its peace.

The march has gone and disappeared.

It metamorphosed into a howl
the wind winnowed.
And now, instead of festive poets here,
the wind will recite into thin air,

it will utter scurrying dust and pulsating heat
above the concrete square.

That our women have been loved seems quite incredible.

Above the era
of taut ropes and white-hot foundries,
the tentative, wary
present – dust settling – hovers.

Above unfinished buildings:
imperial frauds, fantasies.

I no longer believe
what I believed once.
But the fact that I have believed –
that I compel myself
day by day to recall.

And I do not forgive anyone.

Our terrible loneliness
crackles and flakes
like the rust on iron rails in the heat of the sun.

[CW/GG]

Gratitude

The idiotic silence of state holidays
is no different
from that of Catholic Sundays.
People in collective idleness
are even more repellent
than they are when purpose has harnessed them.

Today I will not
in my old ungrateful way
let gratuitous love decay in me.
In the vacuum of streets
what helps me to escape
is the memory of your face and thighs,
your warmth,
the fish-death smell of your groin.

You looked for a bathroom in vain.
The bed was uncomfortable
like a roof ridge.
The mattress smelt of insecticide,
the new scent of your body mingling with it.

I woke to a cannonade
(a round number of years ago
something happened). You were still asleep.
Your glasses, your patent leather bag
on the floor, your dress on the window-catch
hung inside out – so practical.

One strap of your black slip
had slithered off.
And a gentle light was wavering
on the downs of your neck, on your collar-bones,
as the cannon went on booming

and on a spring poking through
the armchair's cover
fine dust was trembling.

[CW/GG]

To Imre Nagy

You were impersonal, too, like the other leaders,
bespectacled, sober-suited; your voice lacked
sonority, for you didn't know quite what to say

on the spur of the moment to the gathered multitude. This urgency
was precisely the thing you found strange. I heard you,
old man in pince-nez, and was disappointed,
not yet to know

of the concrete yard where most likely the prosecutor
rattled off the sentence, or
of the rope's rough bruising, the ultimate shame.

Who can say what you might have said
from that balcony? Butchered opportunities
never return. Neither prison nor death
can resharpen the cutting edge of the moment

once it's been chipped. What we can do, though, is remember
the hurt, reluctant, hesitant man
who nonetheless soaked up
anger, delusion
and a whole nation's blind hope,

when the town woke to gunfire
that blew it apart.

[CW/GG]

To Be Said Over and Over Again

I glance down at my shoe and – there's the lace!
This can't be gaol then, can it, in that case.

[CW/GG]

Christmas 1956

On the twenty-second, at a certain moment
(6.45 a.m.), I, a child of ill omen,
born between Joe S. and Jesus,
become thirteen. It's my last year
of Christmas being a holiday. There's
plenty to eat: the economy of scarcity
was to my Gran as the Red Sea: she crossed over
with dry feet and a turkey. There's a present too –
for me: I control the market still – my one
cousin a mere girl, only four, and I
the last male of the line
(for the time being). Wine-soup, fish, there's everything,
considering we've just come up from the shelter –
where G.F. kept flashing a tommy-gun
with no magazine in it ('Get away, Gabe,' he was told,
'd'you want the Russkies after us?').
Gabe (he won't be hanged till it's lilac-time)
comes in wishing us merry Christmas, there's no
midnight mass because of the curfew;
I concentrate on *Monopoly*, my present –
my aunt got it privately, the toyshops
not having much worth buying. My aunt has come,
in a way, to say goodbye: she's getting
out via Yugoslavia, but at the border (alas)
she'll be left behind, and so (in a dozen years
about) she will have to die of cancer of the spine.

Nobody knows how to play *Monopoly*, so
I start twiddling the knob on our Orion,
our wireless set, and gradually tune in
to London and America, like Mum in '44,
only louder: it's no longer forbidden – yet.
The Christmas-tree decorations, known by heart,
affect me now rather as many years on
a woman will, one loved for many years.
In the morning, barefoot, I'm still to be found
rummaging through the *Monopoly* cards, inhaling
the smell of fir-tree and candles. I bring in
a plateful of brawn from outside, Gran
is already cooking, she squeezes a lemon,
slices bread to my brawn. I crouch on a stool
in pyjamas. There's a smell of sleep and holiday.
Grandad's coughing in what was the servant's room,
his accountant's body, toothpick-thin,
thrown by a fit of it from under the quilt,
Mother's about too, the kitchen is filling up
with family, and it's just as an observer
dropped in the wrong place that I am here:
small, alien and gone cold.

[CW/GG]

In Memoriam: Péter Hajnóczy

1

My simple, singular, old friend is gone:
not to be seen on this restless earth again.
For earth is jealous and will not submit
to sending back one so much part of it.

2

Forgive me for having troubled you.
(As if anyone'd care
a jot for such scruples over there...)
But of those left here so few

phoning me up would find me
so irritable-anxious for their hello:
I'll never meet such another silken buffalo;
though invariably my life is intertwined

with fluffy news, flimsy messages,
logorrhoeic specimens, supernumeraries,
several 'imposing cut-outs', several one-day lays,

and my projects, my pretexts.
Well, rest in peace there: time goes on its way.
That's quite enough rhyming on pain now for one text.

3

I have more and more cravings,
and fewer and fewer days
to tell off to the last one.
By 2030 (a generous estimate)
we shall – with our wives and our enemies,
those who keep eyes on us and those who pant with us –
all of us, all together, all enrich the soil,
the weird deposit bulldozers scoop up out of it.
A child, jubilant, knocks
soil riddled with fine roots out of your eye-socket:
'Dad, can I take this home? Was it a man or a lady?'

4

As regards public-sector cadavers, this year's
crop of corpses has been truly meagre.
The Lionel Longgones and Frank Fuckknowswhos
claim one another, each the other's 'Own Dead'.
Old gourmet of destruction, what a wry face you'd pull
to go through the same self-serchoice menu
for maybe the tenth time.
The populace has been dying
at the usual rate. Those who work, they in the end find bliss.
The latest thing is private mausolea. I find them less and less funny.
You gone, I have taken to browsing
through the deaths column more attentively
and reading the marble ID's they usually have
set up on the resting estates.

The servile soil produces its yews and cypresses,
bells ring, summoning us to follow someone,
on either side of the road there are fat snails
dragging their backs. The priest is about to utter
inanities, the two fat altar boys
fidget like bacon-rind sizzling in the pan.

God gives the sun no cloudy lining,
unmoved he hearkens to his feeble servant,
he beholds the pinky whiteness of women
swaddled in layers of black sweat down to their knickers,
listens to hoarse male singing, sees experts exchanging looks
as they pat into shape the earth-cake decked with flowers. He's trying
to understand something of us. We, dispersing later,
buy savoury nibbles and the Evening News, our ladies'
fine moustaches get sticky with liqueur,
in the tram the widow wobbles, all puffed up –
a busy, white-cuffed paw (her consoler) groping toward her.
We stop off at the (Imitation) Marble Bride and have a few more.
It is all properly done.
I can't tell you much else, Péter. Nothing remarkable
– especially seen from there: through your specks of dust...

[CW/GG]

Electra

What *they* think is it's the twists and turns of politics
that keep me ticking; they think it's Mycenae's fate.
Take my little sister, cute sensitive Chrysosthemis –
to me the poor thing attributes a surfeit of moral passion,
believing I'm unable to get over
the issue of our father's twisted death.
What do I care for that gross geyser of spunk
who murdered his own daughter! The steps into the bath
were slippery with soap – and the axe's edge too sharp.
But that this Aegisthus, with his trainee-barber's face,
should swagger about and hold sway in this wretched town,

and that our mother, like a venerably double-chinned old whore,
should dally with him simpering – everybody pretending
not to see, not to know anything. Even the Sun
glitters above, like a lie forged of pure gold,
the false coin of the gods!
Well, that's why! That's why! Because of disgust, because it all
        sticks in my craw,
revenge has become my dream and my daily bread.
And this revulsion is stronger than the gods.
I already see how mould is creeping across Mycenae,
which is the mould of madness and destruction.

[CW/GG]

Daydreams

Into destruction I would bring
an order whole and classical.
Hope for the good? Out of the question.
Let me die invisible.

Sors bona nihil aliud. To
whoever digs my bones I send
a message: which is, Look how all
God's picture-images must end.

And no there cannot be a heaven,
or else there oughtn't to be one
for, if there were, this plague of love
would still (come what may) go on.

Nor do I want the obverse – hell –
though of that I've had, will have, my bit
(planks beneath the chainsaw wail).

For anything unready, yet
ready too, I lie in the sun:
let the redeeming nowhere come.

[CW/GG]

SZABOLCS VÁRADY

An Objective Outsider, Should One Exist

An objective outsider, should one exist,
a baby born with an adult brain,
or, let us say, the proverbial Martian,
an objective outsider, should one exist,
would hardly understand,
why it should be in his own interest,
in his own and the world's interest,
in the interests of world history, nay, of the universe
that such and such should,
that such and such ought,
that such and such should certainly be advisable

An objective outsider, should one exist,
should there be one such, so as not to understand,
or to understand in this way, this objective outsider
would not after all be wholly objective.

A still more objective outsider might believe instead that,
one from another solar system or fresh from the womb,
limited furthermore by the power of human language – albeit in
         its most primitive form – this most
objective of outsiders might believe,
employing words in their most traditional,
most outmoded sense, might well believe:
nothing more desirable than that the
nothing more advisable than that the
and nothing could be more conformable than that the

The outermost of objective outsiders
from the utmost periphery might think something like this.

But we, who, in a manner of speaking,
do, so to speak, bear the brunt of the matter,
we, the insiders, through necessarily paying attention to
and following closely the pronouncements of our utmost superiors,
have so thoroughly modified our instincts for language
we prioritise the words' secondary meaning,
we who, for lack of an alternative, occupy the territory

cut out for us, and would happily make do with
the not least fortunate of necessary consequences –
who soon will certainly cease to comprehend
the stages of external objectivity,
nor why our noses no longer wrinkle as though we'd like to show
a proper disgust for it, the scent of a metaphor.

[GSz]

Quatrain

I stand in a hole between Will Be and Was
waiting for things to change but nothing does.
The dust will mount for ever. Rain? Unlikely.
Thunder perhaps. But not here, not precisely.

[GSz]

Chairs Above the Danube

The two chairs were not at all ugly
in their way. Shame about the springs
protruding and about the covers
being so hopelessly filthy. But chairs
are chairs are chairs, and these would do the job.
And so we carried them, mostly on our heads,
from Orlay Street, across what used to be known
as Franz Joseph, now Liberty Bridge, right down
to Ráday Street 2, where P then lived
(as his poems of the time will testify).

A chair, or even two, can prove quite useful
in all kinds of ways. *Two poets on the bridge*
bearing chairs on their heads – one could imagine
a picture with that title. I'd like it to be
an objective picture not one of those
visionary things. The two chairs,
it should be clearly understood, are not to be construed
as haloes round our heads. About the middle of the bridge –
without wanting to make a point of it –
we sat down on them. The springs of one chair
stuck out particularly. I can't remember
which of us had it. No matter, what happened later
can't be explained by that. It was a pleasant
summer evening. We lit a cigarette,
enjoying the comfort of our circumstances,
which were a little unusual.

                          The chairs survived
for a while doing respectable service: they were
the chairs at P's place. But naturally one wants
to improve one's lot: so they gave the chairs
to an upholsterer. Then they changed addresses,
the first time because they had to, the next
because they couldn't stand the flat. We tend
to meet less often nowadays. Much has happened since.
G left A (P's wife) and M (the wife of B)
broke up with me, then the second M
(G's wife) abandoned G and came to live
at my place (the Bs too separated
in the meantime). P tried suicide
and spends most of the time in institutions,
not to speak of changes in world politics,
and in any case there's nowhere to sit down.

[GSz]

The Moonlight Gets into Our Heads

The moonlight gets into our heads, no need to force it:
its potent-spirits dribble like a faucet.
Our long faces light up, unwrinkle, mist.
But could we bear it otherwise, unpissed?
It's not just the madness of some horrid unction
composed of bursting ulcers (since pleasure too might
be on tap), nor of simple malfunction,
this anarchy, this chaos of the moonlight.
It's there in me! But what! A thing that can't quite
burst nor spread, some seething inner brew
whose name or substance I may never write.
Time wasted, time we leak away, run through.
A good thing the moon is frozen in its station!
May the attainable bubble down its flue
and offer the dusty soul its flighty salvation.

[GSz]

ISTVÁN BAKA

Franz Liszt Spends a Night Above the Fishmarket

The candle-flame, a feminine blush, blows out
between the closing thighs of night. It's dark.
A discarded hassock soils the room like ink.
That glimmering is God's ceremonial buckler,
the Milky Way. It is now I should hear the Music
of the Spheres, but like root-crop left too long in tilth,
autumnal-sodden, the heavenly host themselves
have mouldered away.
                    It is quiet. All Hungary
is sleeping. The horizon pouts her lips for a kiss,
makes smacking noises in her sleep and drools:
Be thankful you are one of us, dear boy.
I am thankful. But I hope you will not notice
how the gold-braid of my rhapsodies has faded
on your moth-eaten old ceremonial suit,
my poor country. I have scored you into
the Grand Hotel d'Europa and failed to note
your place has been prepared at the kitchen table.
It's all one now. Sleep on, and may your dreams
return the wide sky's kiss. I won't disturb you.
The piano is a sealed coffin; the tedious
flirtation of the candle is snuffed out.
I gaze dumbly at the Milky Way's corrosions,
and down on the square where traders' stalls grow brilliant
with constellations of scales and stink of fish,
a topsy-turvy world where heraldic angels
serve as ingredients for starch or for poteen,
and the red-white-green insignia we sport
on our breast pockets for bull at target practice.

[GSz]

The Mirror Has Broken

The mirror has broken. From its fragments we
may piece together something like a view,
but earth and sky will not be welded – see,
the darkness comes before the night is due.

The view has broken, from its shards somehow
the mirror may be put together yet,
but earth and sky have changed positions now,

the dark has spilled over the day and set.
My shadow lies beside my wife in bed;
who squeezes through the needle's eye will find
himself in hell.

The mirror has broken, from its shards or fragments
some overview or map may yet be jigged
as in a puzzle, where all things have frontiers
but get mixed up in between, in no-man's-land,
where a pin-cushion turns St Sebastian,
the bronze bells melt into artillery
and we slurp a martial music in the pub
through trumpet-coloured beer. We cannot tell
the white-cloaked winter uniforms from snow.

The mirror has broken, the view has also broken,
and whoever tries to put these things together
confuses view with mirror, shard with fragment,
where days are soaked in darkness and low weather,
where women are impregnated by our shadows,
where from the clamour of bells they pour the sound
of long-range cannons with their distant grumbling,
where every season comes in camouflage,
and boots must be pulled on again. No strolling now
across the broken world with unshod feet,
no marching to the martial stench of beer,
the flames are bursting through the needle's eye.

[GSz]

Passing Through

Like someone rudely woken on a winter
morning on a bench at the station, under
a glass roof soaked through by the bloody sun,
who sits up stiffly in the freezing, un-
swept hall, looks round and finds it all too loud,
and can't see what he's doing in the crowd,
or what brought him to this unfamiliar
terminal in the provinces (who are
these people, where have they all sprung from? why
this shoving others aside, this rushing by?)
then a sprinkling of semi-conscious drunks
spills from the doorways, bums with penknives, ranks
of fur-coated babushkas, loiterers,
soldiers on leave, newsboys, wheeltappers, porters,
sad office workers with worn leather cases,
kids selling towels, gypsies with brown faces
and bundles, skiving students, a lunatic
with empty paper bags whose party trick
is bursting them, some tired security toughs
with bullet proof jackets and Kalashnikovs,
unshaven old tramps and an under age
mother, her child screeching into her ribcage,
streetwalkers, cops, street preachers afloat
on rhetoric...from what vast womb or throat
have all these people issued, and why do they
rush blindly at commands from the PA,
why this swarming, what train is it they want,
why do they labour and look so hesitant,
of all this he knows nothing, but watches amazed
as dawn drips blood-grey through that distant glazed
roof and he cannot now remember whether
it was some curse or mission swept him hither,
or where he comes from, nor can he begin
to guess the past his home is swimming in

like someone rudely woken on a winter
morning on a bench at the station under
a glass roof, so was I born, so cold the air,
so hard the wooden bench, not knowing where

and why, not even now, what deadly crime
I have been exiled for, how long the time
till death or pardon come, His will be done
and God decide, so that I may move on.

[GSz]

PÉTER KÁNTOR

What You Need for Happiness

Not much when
you think about it
two people
a bottle of wine
a little cheese
salt, bread
a room
window and door
the rain outside
long stems of rain
and, of course, cigarettes.
But in all these evenings
only once or twice perhaps will everything come together
as sweetly as in the great poems of great poets.
The rest is preparation
afterthought
headache
laughing cramps,
it's no go, but you must,
too much, but not enough.

[GSz]

Inventory

You left me two shirts:
one for summer, one for winter,
one for spring and one for autumn,
one blue, the other blue.

Two shirts and two books:
an In Search of Orpheus,
and a Leaves of Grass,
a Radnóti and a Whitman.

Two shirts and two books.
And a scarf and a cap:
one blue, the other blue.

And two books.
And a Don Giovanni.
And a Bach and a Vivaldi.

Two shirts: two blue ones,
one for summer, one for winter,
one for spring, one for autumn.

[GSz]

How Can I Explain It to You?

How can I explain it to you?
A man doesn't live so his tooth shouldn't ache.
He doesn't work so he should have money enough to lie on the beach.
Is that really why he works?
Is that why he invented the train, the aeroplane, the spaceship?
Is that really why he invented the train, the aeroplane, the spaceship,
so that he may do still more work? So that he can spend more
          time lying on the beach?
Is that why he has his hair cut, so it should grow faster? So he
          can have his hair cut the sooner?
And the train journeys? And the flying?
Do you think these are merely stations on the way to the beach?
And when the golden age comes and there's peace in the world
          and a universal holiday
will we all stretch out on the Dalmatian beach?
And no one have toothache?
Do you think this is what I dream of when I lie on the divan with
          my eyes closed?
Do you?

And who will decipher the cry of the multi-coloured cockatoo?
And why the little red fish keeps quiet in the shallows?
Who will fit together the pieces of things that are forever breaking?
And who will leave everything behind to follow the songthrush of
       his heart?
Who clings to the mirrored wall of smooth ice?
Who climbs the Himalayas?

Who swims in deeper waters without drowning?
And who dies there more beautifully?
Toot-toot-toot…hoots the steam that lifts the lid.
Do you think I smoke because the golden age might be a long
       time coming?

[GSz]

ZSUZSA RAKOVSZKY

Noon

Less than a half-hour since
your skin was on mine, bare,
the spume of love-making still
in the shell of our flesh folds:
my two feet to left and right
flop apart, the Sun pours down
and, winged, the dull heat is swarming
over me, through me, shushing
within in the throbbing red –
it mounts to my womb, as if
in half sleep I were to conceive
twins by two fathers, both
girls, one blonde, one dark:
one of them aches and pulsates,
the other glisters and is not.

[CW/GG]

No Longer

No longer shall I lay my heart open
or strive towards a goal.
This sober July, this sheer madness
that blooms by system and is organised,
burns in each sense as salt burns in a wound.
It is a southern moment: between walls,
beneath bright awnings, among evergreens,
its dark, holy statue stands –
a saint who with mouth caved in must be a hundred.
An ice-cold glance at the world cannot endure
its counterpart: blind face
turned to the moon, hair streaming in the wind:
ecstasy. What is the eye for, if all
its focus is the sky or the dim future?

What is fire for, fever or pale
obsession, thorn or flame?
And what is ultimate love for?
Why should I choose? Why, if it does not exist,
seek heavenly flame, that the winged form
might in time reveal itself from beneath the flesh?
Whatever substance bodily joy was once
made of, it ages ago burned out. Why
a unique hope, rather than ten thousand?
From the net which is our selves, there is no
getting disentangled, no way out, and no
solution: not by undoing the knot,
picking at it, pulling it even tighter,
or vanishing through your own interstices
in the waters of the world.

[CW/GG]

Addict

What's the alternative? What else is there, tell me?
The stuff others use? I see them on buses,
in the street – their faces anxious and flustered, –
and none of them looks as though she were exactly

delirious with joy simply because she's not on
the needle, because she contrives to live
in the blissful knowledge that for five
days in seven she can lug cheese, batter

away at a typewriter or carry a full bedpan.
There are rewards of course: once home
in my cosy flat, in my one and a half rooms,
I could pot geraniums on my balcony,

smooth the ruffles in my carpet, reap
the fruit of my labours. Well one could do worse.
There are real pleasures, spring, summer, the birds
twittering in the branches, cheep, cheep...

And love, of course. The many-splendoured thing.
You know the scene. You're lying on the bed,
staring straight up, nothing in your head
but the bloody phone which doesn't want to ring...

Half-past seven, eight o'clock – the day
stretches out interminably. Whatever
you look at turns caustic, burns like a fever.
One day I told myself: no more. OK,

but assume that he loves me, perhaps even
marries me. What happens then? Pretty soon
we're down to doing it once in a blue moon;
I'm no longer a woman but a cross between

the Virgin Mary and an old biddy with the shakes.
Tell me I'm wrong. It was the same at home.
Why should I put up with it? Must I come
to this? Did I ask to be born, for heaven's sake?

Perhaps I did apply to join the club. But when
did I accept rules which mean you suffer some
sixty, seventy years, and have in that time
the odd enjoyable minute now and then?

So what if I cheat at times, I have no choice.
The game is safe now: the points mount as I score
and win. Cut the cards a dozen times or more,
or flash the bright lights, I still turn up the ace.

And what have I lost? A graceful old age? When
I gently pat the pool, my turbanned tortoise-
head held above the water like some precious
ornament so my make-up shouldn't run,

doing my dutiful fifty lengths per day,
so that my friends may remark, that although I'm
eighty I don't look a day over seventy. Next time
I'm bedbound, dunking my teeth on a tin tray,

fed through a shiny tube from a plastic bag,
while my skin is bluish green around the veins,
and I burn and shrink in fires without flames,
with my nurse well out of earshot, the old hag...

No problem really – my genes and everything
I've done survives me. That should cheer you up
knowing that somehow you don't come to a stop,
though I've read the universe is collapsing

into itself, or is it expanding? Much
the same thing really. It's hard to accept that
not just me, but earth, sky, light, sound, must go zap,
leaving a thin or dense nothing, a big zilch.

Even time will go. But time does not exist
in any case. I know. I saw. As the sun
rose and touched the dripping tap in the kitchen,
it shone like a bird-headed goddess, a crisp

little peardrop dangling from her beak, until,
its patience worn thin by its weight, it gained length
and narrowed and began its feeble descent:
an eternity passed as it hovered, still

before that snap, and I watched and felt something
click into place and I knew it was the world:
that God is joy. In drip and tap it's him, pearled
and perfect, and if you don't know this you know nothing.

[GSz]

New Life

For keeps this time? Why not? The flat, it's true,
is crammed to the hilt with others' history,
but what if it is? Theirs will not be too

different from yours. Some potted greenery
brought in for winter…three, four months swim by
and you don't even notice the scenery:

crash-helmet on the wardrobe, the pleated sky
of a deep-blue fan pinned out against the wall
like a dead bat, on which two pochards fly

skeetering towards the shelf… Puffy, dropsical,
the doorpost is swollen about rusted locks
(flesh round a wedding ring). A faint pall

of dust on the lamp whose little brain box
reflects the light, fire's pallid baby sister.
Is this a kind of vision, or simply how it looks?

*

A couple of years, and you don't even think of moving.
Or you might, but know it's just not on. Your friend,
D, will not move either, but will still be striving

with vibrant Dostoyevsky's soul, and spend
the next five hundred years hunched over the screen
of his word processor; nor will there be an end

of J, the musician, trailing his scores between
the ground floor and the third, not to mention the Pekes
inherited from his girlfriend, trembling, obscene,

up greasy wooden stairs. A's lousy TV freaks
her out, with its constant humming, heads and busts
of terrorists or commentators with El Greco physiques,

grey skulls aflame in interstellar gusts.
True, she might, if the neighbours got her riled,
eventually fix the doorbell, but the mower rusts

in the shed, and our famous 'lawn' grows wild
in winter, every little weed in furious sprout,
as if the bio-clock were running a self-styled

republic, and had surreptitiously winkled-out
an immaculate display of bleeding hearts,
a hard sell of bright shrubs in shameless rout,

crab apple, Japonica, like common tarts
to strut against a swirling February mist,
the anaemic catkins' less effective arts.

Those straggling off-white hordes in the park insist
on being sea-gulls, stiff, triangular,
and not the soft white geese your eyes first promised,

winged spools, awkward in flight. How spectacular
the sun is when it shines...it casts a fleeting halo
of backlight about trees and grass which are

ideas of greenness but real ideas! And oh
how its thoughtful fingers search my rough tweed coat
for tiny bits of fluff that cling like snow...

*

Two, three years, there's no doubt now: unfazed
by sheer excess, by eighteen kinds of mustard,
I've found my favourite cereal, appraised

the various brands of bathsalts, and adjusted
to being nun or nautch-girl, jewel or jade,
eternally fidgeting in Monday's busted

après-festive pallor, or busily parade
my maddening superiority like a sailor who's
been to Hades. I've earned my accolade

by pitting dark experience against the ingénue's
blank innocence. The bellows driving the high
clouds of my vanity might wear out or refuse

to work, but there'd be air enough for them to hover by
till I grew tired and the ever less spectacular
changes of season, or the rain-blurred years' spry

progress offered me a part more in the vernacular:
teacher or housewife, or – why ever not? –
a leader in the struggle for gay rights or the Popular

Front for the Liberation of Animals, with a pot
of paint at the ready, and a razor in my hand
to slash a bourgeois fur: this could be my lot

if a plain existence were denied to me. (And
why should it? Seagulls, fire and catkins
are plain enough, you won't miss them.) To aband-

on your life is a matter of sloughing skins:
the check-out girl at the grocer's, an Albanian
on the game, tries to recall her origins

as a Friesian fisherman, or a lady in Japan
with a little white dog at her heels...Always
there is something...Something beyond the span

of time or space, from which their combined rays
are simply deflected as from bulletproof glass...
some tiny dense trapped particle, something one pays

like an unreturnable deposit, like a compass
pointing beyond endless dark... a needle in a haystack...
Is there such a thing? *Well, is there? Well? I pass.*

[GSz]

Decline and Fall

At last they will disappear, finally just go,
those cinemas and cigarettes named after terms
derived from military history or constitutional law.
The waterworks, machine-tool factories, firms
producing matchboxes that advise you to pursue
a prudent lifestyle, they will vanish too.
Local branches of the catering industry,
chipped teacups, tubular plastic barstools made for short
legs, flat drinks in bottles whose labels sport
sundiscs and oranges as if the real sun had bleached
them both, tables with marble effects and sticky
tops. They'll survive a while, persist like rime
in the coldest microclimate, in random patches,
but when they do eventually go it won't be time
but earth which swallows them, they will flake off

and soak away: anniversaries, occasions of formal
mourning, ersatz occasions that pass for normal:
Mother's Day, Women's Day, Children's Day, Sports Day,
each with its posters scrubbed, peeling away
to reveal a flowering branch or dove, or a block of
numbers pasted across a girl's virginal face,
(as if atoning for a playboy playmate's vast
overthrusting bunny bosom pressing against lace),
all these will fade away, as will the products
of the Totalitarian-Classical, filthy terminals
and waiting rooms, provincial culture halls
with monstrous frescoes and mosaics docked
of odd teeth, showing humanity gathered
in full-throated choirs, celebrating harvests,
or the manufacture of ball-bearings, breasts
heaving in joy at the redemption of leisure
by culture. Not everything has weathered
so well: where are the experiments with white mice
or ferro-concrete? Burst like a balloon,
a thousand pieces exploding in one vast bloom,
or stretching, shrivelling, curling in long flames
resembling, if in nothing else but this,
a contemporary Rome or Babylon's nemesis.
My mass-produced mirror, my pot of jelloid facecream,
my little brown jugs, will not grace a museum,
provide educational outings for family Sundays,
nor will my remains be preserved in an airtight case
or my colour-rinsed curls and protruding eyes
be twisted into a sheath – my speaking likeness
will not be hung on the wall to oversee the moral
welfare of a new generation; indeed, of the wall,
a prefab component of my industrial highrise,
of that whole moon-grey incubator where each block
rots faster than the inner city's overblown baroque,
not a jot will remain. A few turn-of-the-century
public buildings, slices of elephantine
wedding cake, blackened and growing green,
might yet survive, but their bills designed
for the propagation of an ornamental diction
and their six-foot streamers will have declined
and faded, their threadbare carpets rotted
to an ultimate state of dereliction,
and dehydrating yellow leaves of potted

palms perished in civic halls where council
employees, women in business suits, fill
forms, harangue, register marriages,
and rooms where we presented ourselves, signed up
for birth, death or divorce perhaps survive
preserved in memory's indifferent syrup
only while we who lived them are ourselves alive.

[GSz]

Episode

It's hardly worthwhile noting down which door
leads where – in any case I won't be tapping
my way round the angles of this dark corridor
again, seeking a doorknob, wary of waking
who knows who with a creaky floorboard. Why
take especial notice of a stranger's flat anyway?

In the dim glow of the bathroom mirror
I make out cans of sprays, a double row
of toothmugs, and as in the flash of a camera,
myself in agitated outline. Despite this show
of belonging, I'm out of my element,
a foreign body lodged in an alien event,

no more. But even if the postulated soul
is missing, every gesture of the mock
sacrament enacted on that preliminary roll
of tartan – variations on a common stock
of ideas, but so many and so individual –
in other words the whole neckbreaking ritual

works with such a fluent passion that the cursed
heroine can remain in perpetual mute arrest
even if it's the hundredth time and not the first
when, between deep blue sea and prompter's box,
she shakes her terrified incredulous locks
to stare fixedly at the hand across her breast.

[GSz]

They Were Burning Dead Leaves

They were burning dead leaves. Must oozed with scent,
    tar bubbled and blew.
The moonlight glow behind the thistle bent
    like a torn rainbow.

The street was a forest, night slid into the heart
    of deepest autumn.
A guilty music blew the house apart,
    with its fife and drum.

To have this again, just this, just the once more:
    I would sink below
autumnal earth and place my right hand in your
    hand like a shadow.

[GSz]

Wild Night, Wild Night

> *'Wild Nights – Wild Nights!*
> *Were I with thee'*
>   EMILY DICKINSON

Morning, not night – tightfisted
in all things: our eyes
are watching the clock even in bed,
we scramble into clothes, but though we rise

alert, our senses locating routine,
agenda and form, circumstance
dictates to us – our times together have been
a matter of chance,

the odd exceptional moment…tempting providence
to count on such again.
I could take malicious glee in the past tense,
in missed opportunities when

I changed the sheets, or set out drinks for two.
Devising a solution to bluff
us both into one room requires a compromise ever new,
a greenness ever coming into leaf.

To speak of the debt due to passion would
be as ridiculous as one of those 'chic'
old hats decorated with a bowl of fruit
or a stuffed peacock,

enough to raise a snigger. To say OK,
let's give in and separate,
is such a cliché it seems almost new. But who'd pay
the price of it:

our two bodies hungering for each other,
redeemed by consciences in apple-pie
order? And the absence, the loss, would that be no bother?
It'd sting us like a gadfly.

To fabricate a lifestyle from the sheer necessity
of striking a pose
would take greater fanaticism, greater vanity
than we can impose.

So we get by in our moral no-man's-land,
with every reason
to make one harsh decision, or to let things stand,
each according to season.

[GSz]

BÉLA MARKÓ

A Balkan Prayer

In Balkan trains
among their cells of luggage
bitter people sleep.
So many stings crammed into a beehive!
So many deaths huddled together!
In my dreams, so many platforms decked with flowers!
Blood and tears trickle down the window-pane,
the wheels of the train make music
and soon your murderous bees will take to their wings.
I am like a knife dipped in honey
on a white table;
the morning sun is blazing overhead;
your sweetened knives
honeyed stings, these too are aflame.
My God, what did you use me for?
What did my friends use me for?
What are my loved ones using me for?
What are my children using me for?
The world is St Veronica's veil:
rivers, mountains, stars and bloodstains!
Majestic beehives hum,
Balkan trains steeped in filth,
what am I for?
I have lost all my fear.
The day passes,
the landscape passes, night falls
and round me a hundred thousand deaths
rest on each other sprawling.

July 1990

[CW/GG]

A Cannibal Time

This year our bodies will be bitter,
alien flavours are seeping up through them,
so they capitulate –
is this possible?
from water tainted by strontium, from murderous sunlight,
from virulent alkalis and words
we have hitherto selected (my dearest)
our daily nourishment,
our organs have been functioning,
our hearts, lungs and brains
have strained the filth off ceaselessly
and, like tapwater forced
through various purification-devices,
crystalline poems have poured on to my paper,
we were able to love one another,
our lips had not been poisoned,
and while our cells kept changing all the time
the eye, the hand, the forehead and the groin
remained the same,
no child of ours would wear
the features of a gesticulating puppet
on television,
it would wear the face we'd dreamt of,
our parts resisted stubbornly,
no matter that we'd gaped at calves and pigs,
no matter that we'd seen monsters,
God kept on stubbornly moulding
his own image in us,
no matter that we'd drunk vinegar,
no matter that we'd swallowed emetics,
in truth, it was all in vain,
but the body slowly deteriorates,
and the soul also deteriorates,
poems decay too,
for poisons penetrate
the elastic skin of our cells,
the taut membrane of our words, the inside
will come to resemble the outside,
if there is hatred there, let hatred be,
this is the true defeat,

your mouth will taste bitter when you kiss me,
my mouth will be bitter when I kiss you,
my poem will taste bad,
this cannibal time
does not gobble me up, but it will not let me go,
and so we shall wander around here
forever and ever
not fit to be eaten.

[CW/GG]

When It Is Winter

When it is winter, I too appear dead,
I am not alive, but do not die instead,
the rubbish-dump now comes alive, it sparkles,
rich gems among the rotten vegetables,

and like grey marble slabs with their smooth sheen
the cadavers of dead rats there also gleam,
and the stars, trees and people similarly
keep their silence and shine equally,

there is no good or bad amid the waste
but suffering matter that aches though it remains
itself, being held together by the frost,

but when after long winter, the spring starts
and a crack opens in the oppressive night,
will we then blossom, will we fall apart?

[CW/GG]

GÉZA SZŐCS

The Age of Great Receptions

Ah, do you remember that wedding? Between 1970 and 82,
but closer to eighty
do you remember that tremendous reception? Whose was it anyway,
whose wedding? I have an impression it might have been mine,
no: it was certainly mine, my
wedding
or yours? or both of ours? Who
is capable of answering
this now.
We'd have to look out for photographs. But if
they should exist, if
pictures were taken at all of that wedding
(and I believe none were taken)
even then: those pictures are now
hidden in some barely accessible drawer,
beneath a pile of miscellaneous documents. Files,
the children's certificates of baptism, sheets of faded ink:
an ancient pile of love letters
(of 82 or so)
but the pictures
(if they exist)
are earlier; taken (possibly) between about – as I say
75 and 80, and – significantly – we are sitting
next to each other, but at whose wedding? Dear Jesus, at whose
reception? It is not
apparent from the picture! No, because these photos
have never been developed, that is to say they exist
only in negative. And I
cannot make out negatives,
because we look as if
we had both had lime poured
over us
by some barber,
or, as a friend of mine, Gabi T. would say:
we look like Mr and Mrs Snow White.
Who was sitting beside whom? I have an impression we drank
from the same bottle or glass. Can't you remember, love,
whose wedding it was?

I'm going mad.
True, at that time
weddings were all the rage,
the greatest poets (Szilágyi, Nagy) continuously wrote about them,
marriages and brides,
well – I mustn't lose my thread – weddings were so fashionable then
that all our friends were queuing up to be married,
what did we talk about then, there? I don't remember
only that it was very good, that you were very good
I saw your eyes quite close to mine, who
would have thought then that...
Not I. I loved you very much. Still do. Remember the beer?
Perhaps there was no beer. How tired we were by the morning,
when they brought in the...
the usual food one eats at breakfast, on such occasions. It's not
that I am writing about (where was I?) you sit beside me? I wanted
to ask you out for a walk in a familiar wood –
of birches or oaks, near to the reception –
one tree at least must still remain of it,
you remember, something very important happened at the wedding,
what was it,
dear God, have I forgotten? or do I simply not want to speak
            about it?

[GSz]

Distant Breathing

The parcels come and go between Kolozsvár and Wien.
Condensed milk, condensed blood,
meat pâtés a grateful croaking,
condensed weals on a secret sky
        known only to three people,
speech obscures your mouth,
and pretence your cold shivers,
'really, my dears, I manage fine out here'.
Condensed milk, condensed liver.

Suddenly one day the hand locates
the distant pulse at the bottom
of an empty box in an opened package,
the hand,
          and the mouth unknowingly:
'Heavens, they still remember me.'

The Securitate-man tosses in his bed.
A secret obscures the ploughing
and a small ad covers the secret.
Under the bed,
in a green package:
a boxed heart
and heartbeat.

[GSz]

Poem About the Endless Programme

Under our love there is another,
Within the programme
                    another functions;
Within the monsters another monster,
Beneath the law run deeper sanctions –

an underground stream in the stars
that light our lives with their conjunctions:

under our love there is another.
More vibrant, darker, wetter yet.
It pulses and slips between our fingers
and at night kicks off the covers
like a child in a couchette.
                    Off they slip.

One day you too will take a sip
of the wine hid in the wine, and we
will lose ourselves in the endless programmes
of infinite complexity.

[GSz]

GYŐZŐ FERENCZ

Dream and Forgetting

My little girl is afraid to go to sleep.
Repeatedly she'll call me to her bed.
Perspiring gently when her dreams are deep
She trembles when I go to stroke her head.
She wakes so easily, her eyes flick open,
She sits straight up and asks for a drink but can't
Get back to where she was. She can be woken
By a creaking floorboard. We know she wants
Only to be with us, where we are, here,
She knows the hiding place we can't discover
As well as what it is she can't come near.
She says goodnight as if it were for ever.
I sit in darkness, hear her breathing pulse
And slowly find I'm here and there at once.

[GSz]

The Party According to Ramsey's Principle*

How many people should be
Invited to the Ramsey party
So that among the guests there should
Be three at least who know or else
Not know each other?
Assume six people are invited.
One of them, say *John*, will know
Or else not know at least, say, three
Of the five others. If he knows three
And out of the three there are two

---

*Frank Plumpton Ramsey (1904-1930), mathematician, philosopher, economist, made
a lasting contribution to the field of combinatorics; according to his theory, perfect
disorder is impossible, the appearance of disorder depending on the size of the sample
provided.*

(*Mary* and *Paul*) who know each other
(Together with *John*) they form a quorum;
But if they do not know each other
(Only *John*) then, with the others,
They still constitute a quorum,
In so far as at least three
Don't know each other. And should four,
Say, know or else not know
Another person, eighteen guests
Are necessary. More than that
And only an approximate
Estimate is possible, but that
For now will make no difference.
The Ramsey Principle states clearly
That perfect disorder can't exist.
But how many parties must you have
And how many must I attend
Or not attend that I may know
Or not know you. Either I will
Know your guests or not know them.
I know who knows me and I know
Who doesn't, but could we two form
A quorum, just the two of us
While not knowing how *John* gets on
(With *John*) or Mary (with *Mary*) or Paul (with *Paul*)
Or *you* (with *me*) or *I* (with *you*)?
Could we, and if so, how many of us,
Be guests at a Ramsey party
While examining our reflection
So helplessly in the hall mirror?

[GSz]

Someone Is Speaking and Begins Again

I like looking down from the fifth floor.
There, far below, the evening settles down,
A blue veil rises from the river, the air
Is damp. All day it has been raining heavily.
I'm sitting in the room now, concentrating
On someone's voice: a discussion is in progress,
A lecturer and his students are debating
The values of L.A.White. I too address
The question. I hear myself. They look.
That's all for now. He ends. The wind pushes
A single pane of glass half open. The clock
Says half past seven. A neon tube twitches
As we pack away. He starts to speak again.
They go. I go too. Thank you for your attention.

[GSz]

Grey Streak

Ever the present: the past gets modified.
The shrinking (how many?) years are bent
Through faulty glass; I can't see much beyond
My reasons. The chasm between years grows wide
Then narrows quickly; that which is visible
Is subject to chance, is hardly there at all.

And there's nothing to see: the distant hill
Behind half-lowered blinds appears as merely
One grey streak. The airs judders as we
Set off, hurrying elsewhere, on other parallels,
On different occupations. Nothing touches me:
Where shall I go now once I've been set free?

I've tried. I make decisions as I must,
But then in retrospect the whole thing changes,
The vastness of the mackerel sky ranges
Before me, empty, opaque. Reaching the dust
Of the flat countryside, a mirror slices
Like a razor through opposite seat covers.

Always the present. Posts flick by the window,
Points punctuate the clear straight. How many
Directions do branch lines offer? Once I planned
The future that I wanted. Is it any wonder
(And what kind of wonder) that one can't see clear
Through dirty railway windows? Or a year.

[GSz]

NOTES ON THE POEMS

PAGE NO:

23: *Heart Attack in Tihany.* Tihany is a picturesque spa on Lake Balaton; Szabó spent his last years there, in virtual isolation.

29: *Rivers, Fjords, Villages...* A poem written by Illyés in 1940 at the time of Soviet-Finnish war. The two major battles mentioned are from the Napoleonic wars (Waterloo, Wagram) while the third is from Hungarian history (the Battle of Mohi in 1241 in Hungary when the Mongolic invaders dealt a crushing defeat to the army of the Kingdom of Hungary). Petsamo is the Finnish town that was most heavily bombed by the Soviets.

31: *A Sentence About Tyranny*, probably Illyés's most often anthologised poem, was written in the early 1950s at the apogee of Stalinism but was first published only during the Hungarian uprising of 1956.

40: *Welcome to Thomas Mann.* In January 1937 the great German writer Thomas Mann (at that time already an anti-Fascist émigré) visited Budapest and gave a public reading there. Attila József wrote his poem for that particular occasion (Mann read the poem in German translation and found it 'wonderful'). The poem refers to Hans Castorp, the main character in Mann's novel *The Magic Mountain*, and also to the death of the outstanding Hungarian poet and writer, Dezső Kosztolányi (who died in November 1936).

59: *The First Eclogue.* Radnóti learned about Federico García Lorca's fate during a visit to Paris and from then on he consistently identified himself with Lorca, expecting an equally violent death in the impending European war. Like Lorca, he, too, was shot dead (in November 1944).

71: *Western Australia.* One of Faludy's best poems, he memorised it in a punishment cell in the notorious Stalinist labour camp in Recsk in 1952, and only later committed it to paper.

72: *Swedish Rococo.* This poem is about the Swedish poet and song-writer Carl Michael Bellmann (1740-95). Ulla Winblad was the heroine of his main (and very popular) lyrical cycle 'Fredmans epistlar' (1790) which extolls 'the delights of Venus and Bacchus'.

79: *Pest Elegy.* The Royal is a hotel; Emke and New York are fashionable coffee houses in Budapest.

83: *Romanus Sum.* This poem is best understood in a political rather than historical context: it contrasts 'Roman' rationalism (Western Socialist thought) with 'Byzantine', irrational Stalinism. Vas's public rejection of the latter would have had serious consequences in the 1950s when the poem was written – so it was published only many years later.

120: *Harbach 1944.* Pilinszky was not himself confined to a Nazi labour-camp, but as a Hungarian soldier evacuated to Germany he came across slave-workers and starving inmates of POW camps. This poem was written some years after the war, as indeed were all Pilinszky's war poems. Gábor Thurzó, to whom the poem is dedicated, was a Hungarian prose-writer, at one point a close friend of Pilinszky's.

133: *To a Poet.* No major English poet fell near Tobruk. Nemes Nagy either has in mind Keith Douglas (1922-44) who, having fought as a tank commander in North Africa, fell during the Normandy campaign, or Sidney Keyes (1922-43), who died in the Tunisian campaign.

135: *Akhenaton in Heaven.* Egyptian Pharaoh of the XVIIIth Dynasty, Amenophis IV, 'the heretical king of Amarna' called himself 'Akhnaton' after the sun-god Aton.

138: *Squared by Walls.* This poem of Nagy's, published only in 1965, is about the Hungarian uprising of 1956 and his guilt at remaining a mere observer rather than an active participant in these momentous events.

183: *Abda.* The name of the village in Western Hungary where Miklós Radnóti (1909-44) was shot dead by a firing squad in November 1944. See Biographical Notes.

192: *A Visit to Room 104.* 'The great Titus Dugovich scene' refers to the heroic deed of a soldier in John Hunyadi's army who during the siege of Belgrad (1456) threw himself off the castle while clutching a Turk who was about to hoist the Ottoman flag on the castle tower.

195: *Job.* Ivan Mestrović (1883-1962) was a Croatian sculptor, some of whose works are also in British collections.

206: *The Nights of O.E. Mandelstam.* Osip Mandelstam (1891-1938) is one of the great Russian poets of this century. First exiled to Voronezh for a poem written against Stalin, he died later in a Siberian transit camp or labour camp of the Gulag.

213: *To Imre Nagy.* The poem deals with the events of 23 October 1956 and the execution of Nagy in June 1958. On the evening of the 23rd a vast crowd assembled outside the Parliament building in Budapest demonstrating for democratisation and demanding that Nagy (a Reformist Prime Minister in 1953-54) should take over the government. Nagy spoke to the crowd from the balcony of the Parliament in an unsuccessful attempt to calm them down. Soon afterwards he was appointed Prime Minister and on November 1 he declared Hungary's break with the Warsaw Pact. Deposed by Soviet troops on 4 November 1956, he was deported to Romania and eventually tried and hanged 'for treason' in 1958. In 1989 he was fully rehabilitated and reburied in Budapest.

214: *Christmas 1956.* i.e. two months after the uprising. 'Between Joe S. and Jesus': Joseph Stalin was born in December, too.

215: *In Memoriam Péter Hajnóczy.* Péter Hajnóczy (1942-81) was one of the most talented "rebellious" prose-writers of his generation.

223: *Franz Liszt Spends a Night Above the Fishmarket.* Ferenc (or Franz) Liszt (1811-86), the great composer, though spending most of his life in other countries, always considered himself Hungarian. This poem refers to a return to Hungary some time before his decision to settle down in Pest in 1871.

244: *The Age of Great Receptions.* 'The greatest poets' is a reference to Domokos Szilágyi, a Transylvanian Hungarian poet, and to László Nagy, a much-acclaimed poet in Hungary, both personal acquaintances of Szőcs (see Biographical Notes).

BIOGRAPHICAL NOTES

Lőrinc Szabó (1900-57) was born at Miskolc and educated in Debrecen and Budapest. He studied literature and philosophy at the Péter Pázmány University but left without a degree. From the 1920s onwards he worked as a journalist of the *Est-lapok*, while publishing numerous books of poetry and poetic translations. His first collection appeared in 1922; his early poetry can be best described by the emblematic titles of his books: *Kaliban!* (Caliban!) and *A Sátán Műremekei* (The Devil's Masterpieces). His best work is probably the poetic cycles 'Tücsökzene' (Cricket Music) and 'A huszonhatodik év' (The Twenty-Sixth Year) summing up Szabó's life experiences and expressing his grief over the death of a lifelong lover. The rebellious Expressionism of the early years gave way to an ambition to capture the richness and variety of human life, to which end he employed, with great skill, a colloquial variant of the eighteen-line and the Shakespearean sonnet. He translated Villon, Coleridge, Baudelaire and Shakespeare (both the sonnets and several plays) into Hungarian.

Gyula Illyés (1902-83), son of a machine operator at a large Transdanubian estate, comes from mixed Catholic and Protestant peasant stock. His political involvement with the Hungarian Soviet republic of 1919 prompted his emigration to Paris from where he returned to Hungary only in 1926. He became one of the guiding spirits in the movement of the 'village-explorers' and his *Puszták népe* (The People of the Puszta, Engl. tr. G. Cushing), published in 1936, became an influential work revealing the grinding poverty of much of rural Hungary. Illyés wrote poetry throughout his life; his collected poems appeared in two volumes in 1972 and 1973. A winner of the prestigious Baumgarten Prize before the Second World War, he was awarded the Kossuth Prize twice after the war. A talented epic poet at the outset of his career, some of Illyés's lyrical poems – mostly traditional in form and content – became well-known outside Hungary, e.g. his 'One Sentence on Tyranny', a powerful indictment of tyranny of any political colouring, first published during the revolution of 1956. Two collections of Illyés appeared in English: the first edited by Thomas Kabdebo and Paul Tabori was published by Occidental Press in Washington in 1968 (*A Tribute to Gyula Illyés*), while the second was brought out by Chatto and Windus in 1971. Illyés visited Britain several times and the USA once. Apart from poetry and prose, he also wrote historical plays, one of which, *A tiszták* (The Pure Ones), takes its plot from the suppression of the medieval Cathar heresy of Southern France.

Attila József (1905-37), son of an unskilled worker of Romanian origin and of a washerwoman, lost both his parents at an early age: his mother died and the father left the family. Born in Budapest, he studied Hungarian and French literature at the University of Szeged, but after a clash with a conservative professor he left for Vienna and then Paris, never to complete his studies. Although an active member of the illegal Communist Party between 1930 and 1933, his disagreements with the Moscow-inspired Party line both on ideology and on strategy led to an 'expulsion' from the movement. His first book of poetry was published in 1922; six further collections followed, the last of which *Nagyon fáj* (It Hurts Too Much, 1935) sold only a few copies and it was only after his suicide under the wheels of a freight-train at Balatonszárszó that József was recognised as a major poet. The "proletarian" Surrealism of his early poetry was later tempered by a classicism in which he tried to fuse the thought of Hegel, Marx and Freud with often exciting results. His last poetic period, when he became editor of the independent leftist review *Szép Szó*, produced work striking in its linguistic inventiveness and sombre, bold imagery; at the time he was tormented by guilt feelings, by a kind of *Angst* not unlike that of the Existentialists. There are numerous collections of József in English of which *Selected Poems and Texts* (Carcanet, 1973) tr. John Bátki, and *Perched on Nothing's Branch* (Apalachee Press, 1987, 1989, and 1993) tr. Peter Hargitai, had the most critical attention.

Jenő Dsida (1907-38), born at Szatmár (now Satu Mare), was a Transylvanian Hungarian poet of unusual range and sensitivity. Most of his adult life he spent at Cluj (Kolozsvár) where he worked as a journalist. He published only two collections of poetry in his lifetime; the third one *Angyalok citeráján* (On Angelic Zithers) was brought out posthumously in 1938. His poetry oscillates between an enthusiastic affirmation of life and a feeling of approaching doom – the latter probably related to his physical condition, having been troubled since childhood with a serious heart condition. He translated Georg Trakl into Hungarian, as well as the Romanian poet Eminescu, and was influenced by Edgar Allan Poe. His most complete collection of poetry to date was published in 1983 in Hungary.

Miklós Radnóti (1909-44), born in Budapest of a Jewish family, converted to Catholicism in 1943. He lost his mother and twin brother at birth, a fact which left him with a life-long sense of guilt. He studied Hungarian and French literature at the University of Szeged, graduating in 1934, but was unable to find permanent employment as schoolteacher. His first book of poetry *Pogány köszöntő* (A Pagan Salute) was published in 1930. In 1935 he married Fanni Gyarmati and settled in Budapest; he also became a frequent contributor to the leading cultural review *Nyugat*. Radnóti's real stature as poet became apparent only during the Second World War when he managed to articulate the anguish of the threatened and persecuted individual in classical form and created work of great compassion and beauty. In 1944 he was called up to a labour battalion and sent to the labour camp in Bor (Yugoslavia), from where he was evacuated and forced to march towards Germany. When he grew too weak to continue his march, he was shot dead by soldiers accompanying the forced labourers near the village of Abda in Western Hungary. Some of his last poems, published in the posthumous collection *Tajtékos ég* (Foaming Sky, 1946), were found on his body when it was exhumed for reburial after the war. Radnóti is the Hungarian poet most often translated into English. Of the collections available the most critical acclaim was given to *Forced March: Selected Poems* (tr. Clive Wilmer and George Gömöri, Carcanet Press, 1979) and *Foaming Sky* (tr. Frederick Turner and Zsuzsanna Ozsváth, Princeton, 1992); scholars of Radnóti might also find useful *Complete Poetry* (tr. Emery George, Ardis, Ann Arbor, 1980).

György Faludy (1910-) was born and educated at Budapest. He first caused a stir in the 1930s with his colourful paraphrases of François Villon's ballads. A radical Leftist and an anti-fascist, he was forced to leave Hungary in 1938. Two years later he fled from Paris to North Africa and eventually to the United States where he joined the U.S. army and was in service in the Far East. Returning to Hungary in 1946 he worked there as a journalist until his arrest on trumped-up charges in 1950. For three years he was interned in the notorious Gulag-type labour camp at Recsk. In 1956 he emigrated for the second time and lived in London, Malta, and finally Canada. Since 1989 he has been living in Hungary. Faludy's image-laden and accessible poetry was influenced by Heine and Brecht and by some Hungarian poets of the first *Nyugat* generation; the sensuous abandonment of his early poetry gradually changed to a sparser, more philosophical mood in the 1960s. His autobiography *My Happy Days in Hell* (London, 1962) is most entertaining. Faludy's poetry was translated by a number of Canadian poets, the latest selection being *Selected Poems by George Faludy* (ed. and tr. by Robin Skelton, University of Georgia Press, Athens, 1985).

István Vas (1910-91) was born in a bourgeois family in Budapest. He studied at a business academy in Vienna where he met Etel Nagy, his first wife (she was stepdaughter to Lajos Kassák, the dominant figure of the Hungarian Avant-garde). The young Vas also published his poetry in Socialist-leaning Avant-garde reviews, but by the time his first book *Őszi rombolás* (Autumnal Destruction, 1932) was published he had returned to a more traditional, classical model of poetry. A clerk before World War II, Vas worked for a publishing house from 1946. In 1951 he married his post-war companion, the painter Piroska Szántó. Vas's collected poems *Mit akar ez az egy ember?* (What Does This One Person Want?) were published in two volumes in 1970. He visited Britain several times and was an excellent translator of English poetry (Shakespeare, Donne, T.S. Eliot); his autobiographical trilogy (1964-81) established him as a consummate writer of prose. He was translated into English by several poets, most of whom contributed to the collection *Through the Smoke: Selected Poems*, ed. Miklós Vajda (Corvina, 1989).

László Kálnoky (1912-85) was born in Eger, and educated at Eger, Budapest and Pécs. He was a minor government official before the Second World War and editor in a publishing house between 1954 and 1957. His first book of poetry came out in 1939 and his *Collected Poems* in 1980. He was a prolific translator of both poetry and drama, the latter including translations of Marlowe and Goethe. Kálnoky's early poetry follows the poetic models of the first generation of *Nyugat*: over sixty his poetry gained a new lease of life and amazed critics with its Surrealist imagery and wry humour. Some of his poems were translated by Edwin Morgan and appeared in the *New Hungarian Quarterly*.

Sándor Weöres (1913-88) was born in Szombathely, near the Austrian border and lived in a small village where his father owned an estate. He studied law, then philology at the University of Pécs in Southern Hungary. His first book of poetry was published in 1934 and in 1936 he won the Baumgarten Prize. He travelled in Europe and in the Far East in the late 1930s; in the next decade he was librarian first at Pécs, then Székesfehérvár and finally in Budapest. His poetry, blending ancient myths with a playful or ironic handling of everyday human situations, blossomed during and after the Second World War but he was branded a 'Nihilist' by Marxist critics and for a while could make a living only with his poetry for children and verse translations. His collection *A hallgatás tornya* (The Tower of Silence, 1956) established Weöres as one of Hungary's foremost modern poets. His astounding range and great mastery of the language eventually brought him official recognition: in 1970 he was awarded the Kossuth Prize. He visited Britain several times and had a selection of his poetry translated by Edwin Morgan already in 1970 – this was published in a Penguin paperback shared with Ferenc Juhász. In 1988, however, *Eternal Moment*, a representative selection from his work was published by Anvil/Corvina; this was edited by Miklós Vajda and translated by several poets including George Szirtes, Hugh Maxton and Edwin Morgan.

Zoltán Jékely (1913-82) was born in Nagyenyed (now Aiud) in Transylvania. He was educated in Cluj (Kolozsvár) and at Budapest. From 1935 to 1941 he worked in the Hungarian National Library and between 1941 and 1946 lived once again in Cluj, where he was first a librarian then a journalist. He moved back to Hungary in 1946. Jékely's début took place in 1936 and in 1939 he won the Baumgarten Prize, but his 'apolitical' poetry was disapproved by the Communist overseers of culture, so he had to wait until 1957 for the publication of his *Selected Poems*. He was an excellent translator of Dante, Shakespeare and Goethe, and the author of several historical plays.

Győző (in its anglicised form, **Victor**) **Határ** (1914-) was born in Gyoma and educated in Budapest where he completed his studies in architecture in 1938. During World War Two his long satirical novel *Csodák országa Hátsó-Eurázia*, ready for publication, was impounded at the printer's; he was jailed for five years for anti-war propaganda. In 1950 he tried to leave Hungary illegally for which he was sentenced to a jail term of two and a half years. After his release he worked first as an architect and later as a translator of foreign literature. He left Hungary in 1956 and came to Britain where he found work in the Hungarian section of the BBC until 1976. In 1991 he was awarded the Kossuth Prize. Határ is one of the most prolific Hungarian men of letters. He has produced valuable work in all genres, most notably in his plays which are steeped in philosophy and historiosophy, collected in the two volumes of *Sirónevető* (Laughing-Crying, Munich, 1972). The first major selection of his poems, *Hajszálhíd* (A Bridge of Hair, Munich, 1970) comprises work which was unpublishable in Communist Hungary. Another important selection of his poetry entitled *A léleknek rengése* (The Quake of the Soul) was brought out in Budapest in 1990. The range of his poetry is unusually wide, it comprises Avant-garde experiments and Surrealistic texts as well as post-romantic rhyming quatrains and couplets.

János Pilinszky (1921-81) was born and educated in Budapest, studying first law, then philology. His first poems appeared in literary reviews as early as 1940. Towards the end of the war he was drafted into the Hungarian Army, and evacuated with his unit to Germany but he made his way back from there in 1945. After various editorial jobs in 1957 he became a member of staff on the Catholic weekly *Új Ember*, a position he held until his death. In the 1960s and 70s he travelled widely in Europe, spending long periods in France and visiting Britain several times. His slim collection *Harmadnapon* (On the Third Day, 1959) established his reputation as one of the leading poets of his generation; his tormented, existentialist Catholicism found expression is sparsely worded, haunting poems about human suffering. His collected poems were published as *Kráter* (Crater, Budapest, 1976). In 1980 he was awarded the Kossuth Prize. There are three collections of his poetry available in English: *Selected Poems* (Carcanet, 1976), tr. Ted Hughes and János Csokits; *Crater: Poems 1974-75*, tr. Peter Jay (Anvil, 1978) and *The Desert of Love* (an extended edition of the 1976 collection; Anvil, 1989). Pilinszky's conversations with the black American actress Sheryl Sutton were published in 1992 by Carcanet/Corvina (*Conversations with Sheryl Sutton*, tr. Peter Jay and Eva Major.)

Ágnes Nemes Nagy (1922-91) was born in Budapest. She studied Hungarian and Latin at university. For some years she was on the staff of an educational magazine; from 1953 to 1958 taught in a secondary school; after 1958 she supported herself from her writing. She translated much from German and French, also from English; in the late 1970s she and her husband, the critic Balázs Lengyel spent several months on a Writers' Visiting Fellowship at the University of Iowa. She was associated with the post-war literary review *Újhold* (New Moon) banned in 1948, and with the trend of objective poetry which severely curtailed the role of the 'lyrical ego' in the poem. In 1983 she was awarded the Kossuth Prize. Two selections of her poetry are available in English: *Selected Poems*, tr. Bruce Berlind, Iowa, 1980, and *Between*, tr. Hugh Maxton, Corvina, 1989. A selection of her poems translated by George Szirtes, is in preparation for publication by Oxford University Press in 1997.

László Nagy (1925-78) was born at Felsőiszkáz in Western Hungary of peasant stock. From 1946 he lived at Budapest where he first studied to become a painter but in 1948 changed over to philology and philosophy and eventually to Russian language. From 1949 to

1952 he lived in Bulgaria on a writer's scholarship and was influenced by Bulgarian folk art. From 1953 to 1956 he was on the staff of a children's paper and from 1959 worked for the weekly *Élet és Irodalom*. His first book of poetry appeared in 1949 but his best work went into the collections *Deres majális* (Frosty Fair in May, 1957) and *Himnusz minden időben* (Hymn at Anytime, 1965) where he combined the tradition of folk-poetry and of Romanticism with modernistic imagery and symbols of universal relevance. He translated extensively from a number of languages, including the work of Federico García Lorca and Dylan Thomas with whom he felt an affinity. His selected poems were published in English in 1973: *Love of the Scorching Wind*, ed. George Gömöri and Gyula Kodolányi (Oxford University Press/Corvina); apart from Tony Connor and Kenneth McRobbie he was also translated by Edwin Morgan and Alan Dixon.

László Lator (1927-) was born in a village in South-Eastern Hungary, was educated at Makó and studied Hungarian and German philology at Budapest. For some time he taught in a provincial secondary school, but since 1955 he has worked as editor in a Budapest publishing house. An excellent translator of poetry from many languages, Lator is also an eminent critic. His first book of poetry was published only in 1969. In 1995 he was awarded the Kossuth Prize. English translations of some of his poems appeared in the *Hungarian Quarterly*.

Ferenc Juhász (1928-) was born in a village near Budapest, the son of a stonemason. From 1948 to 1951 he studied philology at the University of Budapest (ELTE) but took no degree. From 1951 to his retirement he worked for a Budapest publishing house; he was also a contributor and later (from 1974 to its cessation) editor of the literary monthly *Új Irás*. He was awarded the Kossuth Prize twice, in 1951 and in 1973. Juhász's poetry is neo-romantic, although some critics regard him as an unbridled Expressionist on the grounds of the volcanic power of his imagery which attempts to capture not only the mystery of life but that of cosmic creation. His best work pre-dates 1965 when he brought out the collection *Harc a fehér báránnyal* (Struggle with the White Lamb); this includes the long poem 'The Boy Changed into a Stag' which greatly impressed W.H. Auden. Since then Juhász has added twenty-odd further titles to his list, but his poetic reputation has not improved. There are two collections of his work in English: *The Boy Changed into a Stag: Selected Poems 1949-1967*, tr. Kenneth McRobbie and Ilona

Duczynska, OUP, Canada, 1970, and a paperback volume shared with Weöres: *Selected Poems*, tr. David Wevill, Penguin Modern European Poets, 1970.

Sándor Kányádi (1929-) is a native of Transylvania and has lived since 1950 at Cluj (Kolozsvár) in Romania. He studied Hungarian philology at the then autonomous Bolyai University and graduated in 1954. He has worked for various journals since, and has spent many years on the staff of the Hungarian-language children's magazine *Napsugár*. His first book of poetry was published in 1955 but it was only in the 1960s that he found that distinctive voice which expresses the fears and endeavours of the Hungarian ethnic minority in Romania as well as the sense of displacement of an intellectual from a rural community. In the 1980s when his poetry (other than children's verse) could not be printed in Romania, his books were published in Hungary. In 1993 he was awarded the Kossuth Prize in Hungary, and in 1995 the Austrian Herder Prize.

Sándor Csoóri (1930-) comes from peasant stock. He was educated at Pápa and Budapest. He studied Russian at the latter but did not complete his studies. His first book of poetry appeared in 1954 and thanks to the more liberal atmosphere ushered in by Imre Nagy's first government, it could include poems critical of the previous Stalinist régime. He worked as a journalist on the staff of various papers; after 1968 he was script reader and artistic adviser for a Budapest film studio (MAFILM). Since 1988 he has been Editor-in-Chief of the cultural review *Hitel* and in 1991 was elected President of the World Federation of Hungarians. He has also published several much acclaimed and one politically controversial collections of essays. In his poetry Csoóri is a post-Romantic 'imagist' whose lyrical confessions are related to a particular strain in the Hungarian poetic tradition. Several collections of his poetry are available in English: *Memory of Snow*, tr. Nicholas Kolumban (Penmaen Press, Great Barrington, 1983); *Barbarian Prayer: Selected Poems* (tr. by various hands, Corvina, 1989); and *Selected Poems* (tr. Len Roberts, Copper Canyon Press, 1992).

László Marsall (1933-) was born and educated in Budapest. He studied mathematics and physics at University but did not complete his studies. He has worked for the Hungarian Radio since 1957. He is the only genuine Surrealist of the post-war generation though his fondness for the grotesque and the bizarre sometimes give way to a passionate commitment to sensual love. His first book of poetry *Vízjelek* (Watermarks) was published in 1970, since when four more of his collections have appeared. In 1984 he won the Attila József Prize.

Elemér Horváth (1933-) was born at Csorna near the Austrian border and was educated at the Benedictine school of Pannonhalma. He left Hungary in 1956, continuing his studies in Italy but not taking a degree. Since 1962 he has been living in Mahopac, New York State, where he works as a printer. His first book of poetry *A mindennapok arca* (The Face of Everydays) was published in Rome in 1962. Some of his poems were published in *The Hungarian Quarterly*. In 1992 he won the Graves Prize in Hungary.

György (George) Gömöri (1934-) was born in Budapest, educated at Budapest, Sárospatak and Oxford. He studied Polish and Hungarian literature at the University of Budapest (ELTE) but left Hungary after the 1956 uprising. After studies in Oxford he travelled and taught in the United States. Since 1969 he has been teaching Polish and Hungarian at the University of Cambridge. His collections of poetry appeared in London, Munich and Washington D.C. but only the sixth of these, *Búcsú a romantikától* (Farewell to Romanticism, 1990), could be published in Hungary. With Clive Wilmer he has translated many Hungarian poets into English. In 1993 he won the first Salvatore Quasimodo Memorial Prize for Poetry and in 1995 the Italian poetry prize 'In the Footsteps of Ada Negri' (Lodi).

László Bertók (1935-) was born in a Transdanubian village and was educated at Csurgó. In 1955 he was briefly jailed for poems which entailed 'political incitement'. For a while he did physical work, then studied at the Academy of Pedagogy at Pécs from where he graduated in 1963. Later he studied librarianship at Budapest. From 1977 to 1982 he was Director of the Town Library at Pécs and since 1975 a member of the editorial staff of the Pécs review *Jelenkor*. He won a number of literary prizes, including the Graves Prize (1989) and the Tibor Déry Award (1990).

Ottó Orbán (1936-) was born and educated in Budapest. He studied Hungarian philology and librarianship at University but did not complete his degree. Since 1960 he has worked as a freelance writer and from 1981 he has been on the staff of the literary review *Kortárs* in Budapest. He has translated extensively from a number of languages, including English and American Beat poets. He visited the United States several times, and in 1987-88 taught there as Guest Professor at the University of Minnesota. He was awarded the Kossuth Prize in 1992. A collection of his poetry in English was published by Bloodaxe and Corvina: *The Blood of the Walsungs: Selected Poems*, ed. George Szirtes, tr. various hands, Newcastle, 1993.

Domokos Szilágyi (1938-76). Transylvanian Hungarian poet, was educated in Satu Mare (Szatmárnémeti) and lived from 1955 at Cluj (Kolozsvár) where he completed his studies at the Babes-Bolyai University. In 1958-59 was on the staff of the review *Igaz Szó* and from 1960 onwards was on the staff of the Hungarian-language Bucharest daily *Előre* until his retirement on grounds of health in 1970. In his last years he lived at Kolozsvár. Szilágyi's first book of poetry was published in 1962 but only the collection *Búcsú a trópusoktól* (Farewell to Tropics, 1969) established him as one of the best poets of his generation. He translated Walt Whitman and modern Romanian poets and tried to combine in his work the traditions of Hungarian poetry with the formal innovations of the Avant-garde.

Zsuzsa Takács (1938-) studied Spanish and Italian literature at the University of Budapest (ELTE). For a while she worked as Lectrice at Havana University in Cuba. Since 1964 she has been teaching Spanish at the University of Economics in Budapest. She won the Graves Prize in 1984 and the Déry Award in 1990. Her poems appeared in English in the *Hungarian Quarterly*, translated by George Szirtes.

Dezső Tandori (1938-) was born and educated in Budapest. He studied Hungarian and German at the University of Budapest (ELTE) and was a lecturer until 1971, since when he has been a freelance writer and translator. He has travelled extensively in Europe, visiting most racecourses on the continent and in Britain. He has won a number of awards, the most prestigious of which are the Graves Prize (1972) and the Sándor Weöres Prize (1990). He has translated from many languages, including modern English and American authors (Salinger, Wallace Stevens, e.e. cummings, John Berryman, Virginia Woolf). His first book *Töredék Hamletnek* (Fragment for Hamlet, 1968) was an interesting attempt to reduce poetry to its most essential components, whereas his next collection *Egy talált tárgy megtisztítása* (Cleansing of a Found Object, 1973) was hailed by some critics as 'the first postmodern collection in Hungary' because of its wide range of themes and formal experimentation. On the one hand Tandori insists on writing about his private world (which is mainly populated by highly individual sparrows), on the other hand he plays down the 'poetic' element of poetry by producing ephemeral and prosaic texts about practically anything that comes to his mind. He has written a number of perceptive essays and garrulous novels. A collection of his poetry was published in a bilingual (English/Hungarian) edition by Bruce Berlind: *Birds and Other Relations: Selected Poetry* (Princeton, 1986).

István Bella (1940-) was born and went to school at Székesfehérvár. Studied Hungarian and librarianship at the University of Budapest (ELTE) but did not complete his studies; instead he started working as librarian at the Faculty of Law. There he edited the university review *Tiszta szívvel*. Between 1965 and 1968 he worked as librarian in a factory. In 1969 he spent a year on a scholarship of the Writers Association in Poland. From 1978 he has been on the staff of the literary journal *Élet és Irodalom*, and more recently *Magyar Napló*. A long poem of his was included in the collection *Homage to Mandelstam*, ed. Richard Burns and George Gömöri (Cambridge, 1980).

György Petri (1943-) was born and educated in Budapest. From 1966 to 1971 he studied Hungarian and philosophy at the University of Budapest (ELTE). His first book of poetry was published in 1971 and his next collection in 1974, but between 1977 and 1989 he could not publish his politically outspoken poetry in the literary press, only in *samizdat*. After three small *samizdat* collections which paradoxically enhanced his popularity in Hungary and abroad, in 1989 a Budapest publisher brought out a wide selection of his work, *Valahol megvan* (Somewhere It Exists) which since has been followed by other collections. In 1990 he was awarded the Attila József Prize, and in 1996 the Kossuth Prize. Petri's is a distinctive new voice in Hungarian poetry: his grotesque, often bitterly sardonic approach to conventional values is coloured by a strange fascination with death. In Britain, Bloodaxe have published a selection of Petri's work: *Night Song of the Personal Shadow: Selected Poems*, tr. Clive Wilmer and George Gömöri (Newcastle, 1991).

Szabolcs Várady (1943-) was born and educated in Budapest. First he worked as corrector for a Budapest publishing house, and in 1969 graduated at the Faculty of Philology of the University of Budapest (ELTE). From 1971 to 1989 he was editor for the Európa Publishing House and since 1989 has been on the staff of the literary monthly *Holmi*. He has translated English and American poetry. Várady is a laconic and ironic poet, since his début in the anthology *Első ének* (1968) he has published only two books of poetry, but has won a number of literary awards, including the Graves Prize (1981) and the Tibor Déry Award (1987).

István Baka (1948-95) was born and went to school in Szekszárd. He studied Russian language and literature at Szeged (JATE). Since 1974 he has been on the staff of the Szeged-based children's magazine *Kincskereső*, and Deputy Editor since 1993. He has published six collections of poetry and several books of stories. His poetry has affinities with modern Russian poets, many of whom he has translated into Hungarian. He has won a number of literary awards including the Graves Prize (1985), the Attila József Prize (1989) and the Tibor Déry Award (1993).

Péter Kántor (1949-) was born and raised in Budapest. He first studied languages (English and Russian) and later Hungarian at the Faculty of Philology of ELTE. He has been in turn a schoolteacher, a translator and a freelance writer. He has visited Britain and the United States several times. He has edited an anthology of contemporary British poetry. English translations of his poems by George Szirtes appeared in the *New Hungarian Quarterly*.

Zsuzsa Rakovszky (1950-) was born in Sopron near the Austrian border. She went to school there, continuing her studies at Budapest where she graduated in Hungarian and English in 1975. For a while she worked as a librarian, and, between 1982 and 1986, as a reader for the Helikon Publishing House. Since 1986 she has been a freelance poet and translator. She spent a year in London on a poetry scholarship and was a guest of Poetry International in 1994. She has twice won the Tibor Déry Award and in 1988 the Attila József Prize. She was one of several poets represented in the anthology *Child of Europe*, ed. Michael March (Penguin Books, 1990). Since then her work has been included in a small collection published for the 1991 Cheltenham Festival *As if...* (The Starwheel Press, 1991), shared with two other Hungarian poets. In 1994 Oxford University Press brought out *New Life*, a selection of her work translated by George Szirtes, for which he won the European Poetry Translation Prize.

Béla Markó (1951-) is a Transylvanian Hungarian poet, born in Seklerland. He studied Hungarian and French literature at the Babes-Bolyai University in Cluj (Kolozsvár). He has been on the staff of the Tirgu Mures (Marosvásárhely) literary review *Igaz Szó* for many years, and since 1989 has been Editor of its successor *Látó*. In 1993 he was elected President of the Democratic Union of Hungarians in Romania. His first book of poetry was published in 1974; some of his poems have appeared in English in *The New Hungarian Quarterly*.

Géza Szőcs (1953-) was born at Tirgu Mures (Marosvásárhely), and studied Hungarian and Russian at the University Babes-Bolyai at Cluj (Kolozsvár). In 1979-80 he was in Vienna on a literary scholarship. In the 1980s he edited the samizdat publication *Ellenpontok* and as a result of his political opposition to the Ceaucescu régime in 1986 was forced to emigrate. He lived in Switzerland until 1990 when he returned to Romania where he was elected Senator to the Romanian Parliament and Secretary General of the Democratic Union of Hungarians in Romania. Since 1992 he has been director to a publishing company. He has won the Graves Prize (1986), the Tibor Déry Award (1992) and the Gábor Bethlen Prize (1993). Since his début in 1975 Szőcs has published nine collections of poetry, partly in Romania, partly abroad.

Győző Ferencz (1954-) was born and educated in Budapest where he studied English and Hungarian at ELTE. In 1982 he received a doctorate in literature. From 1982 for ten years he was editor in the Europa Publishing House; recently he has been teaching English Literature at the University of Budapest. From 1989 to 1991 he was editor of the *Újhold* Yearbook. He translates English and American poets; he won the Graves Prize (1987) and the Tibor Déry Award (1990). In 1991 he was guest of the Cheltenham Festival and some of his poems appeared in the collection *As if...* (The Starwheel Press, 1991) which he shared with two other Hungarian poets.

ACKNOWLEDGEMENTS

Acknowledgements are due to the following translators, editors and publishers:

Lőrinc Szabó: tr. Edwin Morgan.

Gyula Illyés: tr. Donald Davie (by permission of the Estate of Donald Davie), Charles Tomlinson and William Jay Smith from *Modern Hungarian Poetry*, ed. M. Vajda (Columbia University Press, New York, 1977); tr. Christine Brooke-Rose from *A Tribute to Gyula Illyés*, ed. P. Tábori and T. Kabdebo (Occidental Press, Washington, D.C., 1968).

Attila József: tr. Edwin Morgan from *Sweeping out the Dark* (Carcanet Press, 1994); tr. Vernon Watkins (by permission of Gwen Watkins) from Attila József, *Poems* (The Danubia Book Co., London, 1966); tr. Lucas Myers with Agnes Vadas, *The Hungarian Quarterly*, Nr. 134.

Miklós Radnóti: from Miklós Radnóti, *Forced March: Selected Poems*, tr. Clive Wilmer and George Gömöri (Carcanet Press, 1979); and tr. Zsuzsanna Ozsváth and Frederick Turner from Miklós Radnóti, *Foamy Sky: The Major Poems of Miklós Radnóti* (Princeton University Press, 1992).

György Faludy: tr. Robin Skelton, Eric Johnson, from George Faludy, *Selected Poems*, ed. Robin Skelton (University of Georgia Press, Athens, Georgia, 1985).

István Vas: tr. Donald Davie from *Modern Hungarian Poetry*, ed. M. Vajda (Columbia University Press, New York, 1977), by permission of the Estate of Donald Davie; tr. George Szirtes from Istvan Vas, *Through the Smoke* (Corvina, Budapest, 1989).

Sándor Weöres: 'The Colonnade of Teeth', 'De Profundis', 'Queen Tatavane', 'Monkeyland', 'Ars Poetica' and 'The Lost Parasol', translated by Edwin Morgan, are taken from *Eternal Moment* by Sándor Weöres published by Anvil Press Poetry in 1988; 'Fresco of the 20th Century'; tr. Richard Lourie from *Tri-Quarterly*, 9, Spring 1967.

János Pilinszky: 'Complaint', 'By the Time You Came', 'Harbach 1944', 'On the Wall of a KZ-Lager', 'November Elysium', 'Fable', 'Epilogue', 'Apocryhpha', 'Quatrain' and 'Enough', translated by Ted Hughes and János Csokits, are taken from *The Desert of Love* by János Pilinszky published by Anvil Press Poetry in 1989.

Ágnes Nemes Nagy: from Ágnes Nemes Nagy, *Selected Poems* tr. Bruce Berlind (The University of Iowa, Iowa, 1980) and from Ágnes Nemes Nagy, *Between*, tr. Hugh Maxton (Corvina, 1989).

270 ACKNOWLEDGEMENTS

László Nagy: tr. Tony Connor with George Gömöri from László Nagy, *Love of the Scorching Wind* (Oxford University Press, 1973).

Ferenc Juhász: from Sándor Weöres/Ferenc Juhász, *Selected Poems* (Penguin Books, 1968) and from Ferenc Juhász, *The Boy Who Changed into a Stag: Selected Poems 1949-1967* (Oxford University Press, Toronto, 1970).

Sándor Kányáde: tr. Gerard Gorman.

Sándor Csoóri: from Sándor Csoóri, *Barbarian Prayer* (Corvina, Budapest, 1989) and Nicholas Kolumban, *Turmoil in Hungary* (New Rivers Press, St Paul, 1982).

Elemér Horváth: from Nicholas Kolumban, *Reception at the Mongolian Embassy* (New Rivers Press, 1987); tr. Clive Wilmer and George Gömöri from *Klaonica: Poems for Bosnia*, ed. Ken Smith and Judi Benson (Bloodaxe Books/*The Independent*, 1993); tr. William Jay Smith from *The New Hungarian Quarterly*, No.130.

György Gömöri: from George Gömöri, *My Manifold City* (The Alba Press, 1996).

Ottó Orbán: tr. Edwin Morgan and George Szirtes from Ottó Orbán, *The Blood of the Walsungs: Selected Poems* (Bloodaxe Books, 1993).

Dezső Tandori: tr. Tony Connor from *Ocean at the Window*, ed. Albert Tezla (Minnesota University Press, Minneapolis, 1980); tr. Bruce Berlind from *Selected Poems*, tr. Bruce Berlind (Princeton University Press, 1986, and *The New Hungarian Quarterly*, No.131.

István Bella: from *Homage to Mandelstam*, eds. Richard Burns and George Gömöri (Los, Cambridge, 1980.

György Petri: from György Petri, *Night Song of the Personal Shadow: Selected Poems* (Bloodaxe Books, 1991), and 'Daydreams' from Clive Wilmer, *Selected Poems* (Carcanet Press, 1995).

Zsuzsa Rakovszky: tr. Clive Wilmer and George Gömöri from *Child of Europe*, ed. Michael March (Penguin Books, 1990); tr. George Szirtes from Zsuzsa Rakovszky, *New Life* (Oxford University Press, 1994).

Győző Ferencz: tr. George Szirtes from *As If... Three Hungarian Poets* (The Starwheel Press with the Cheltenham Festival of Literature, 1991).

Every effort has been made to trace copyright holders of material included in this book. The editors and publisher apologise if any material has been included without permission or without the appropriate acknowledgement, and would be glad to be told of anyone who has not been consulted.